Petr Polevoi, R. Nisbet Bain

Russian Fairy Tales

Petr Polevoi, R. Nisbet Bain

Russian Fairy Tales

ISBN/EAN: 9783743307117

Manufactured in Europe, USA, Canada, Australia, Japa

Cover: Foto ©ninafisch / pixelio.de

Manufactured and distributed by brebook publishing software (www.brebook.com)

Petr Polevoi, R. Nisbet Bain

Russian Fairy Tales

RUSSIAN FAIRY TALES

SELECTED AND TRANSLATED FROM

THE *SKAZKI* OF POLEVOI

BY

R. NISBET BAIN

ILLUSTRATED BY C. M. GERE

London
LAWRENCE AND BULLEN
16 HENRIETTA ST., W.C.
1892.

PREFACE.

THE existence of the Russian *Skazki* or *Märchen* was first made generally known to the British Public some twenty years ago by Mr. W. R. S. Ralston in his *Russian Folk Tales*. That excellent and most engrossing volume was, primarily, a treatise on Slavonic Folk-Lore, illustrated with admirable skill and judgment, by stories, mainly selected from the vast collection of Afanasiev, who did for the Russian what Asbjörnsen has done for the Norwegian Folk-Tale. A year after the appearance of Mr. Ralston's book, the eminent Russian historian and archæologist, Peter Nikolaevich Polevoi (well known, too, as an able and ardent Shaksperian scholar), selected from the inexhaustible stores of Afanasiev some three dozen of the Skazki most suitable for children, and worked them up into a fairy tale book which was published at St. Petersburg in 1874, under the title of *Narodnuiya Russkiya Skazki* (Popular Russian Märchen). To manipulate these quaintly vigorous old-world stories for nursery purposes was, as may, well be imagined, no easy task, but, on the whole, M. Polevoi did his work excellently well, and while softening the crudities and smoothing out the occasional roughness of these charming stories, neither injured their simple texture nor overlaid the original pattern.

It is from the first Russian edition of M. Polevoi's book that the following selection has been made. With the single exception of "*Morozko*," a variant of which will be familiar to those who know Mr. Ralston's volume, none of these tales has seen the light in an English dress before; for though both Ralston and Polevoi drew, for the most part, from the same copious stock, their purposes were so different that their selections naturally proved to be different also.

As to the merits of these Skazki, they must be left to speak for themselves. It is a significant fact, however, that all those scholars who are equally familiar with the Russian Skazki and the German Märchen, unhesitatingly give the palm, both for fun and fancy, to the former.

R. N. B.

CONTENTS.

	PAGE
THE GOLDEN MOUNTAIN	1
MOROZKO ...	8
THE FLYING SHIP ...	13
THE MUZHICHEK - AS - BIG-AS - YOUR - THUMB- WITH-MOUSTACHES- SEVEN-VERSTS-LONG	22
THE STORY OF THE TSAREVICH IVAN, AND OF THE HARP THAT HARPED WITHOUT A HARPER	34
THE STORY OF GORE-GORINSKOE	56
GO I KNOW NOT WHITHER—FETCH I KNOW NOT WHAT	64
KUZ'MA SKOROBOGATY	85
THE TSAREVNA LOVELINESS-INEXHAUSTIBLE	94
VERLIOKA	111
THE FROG-TSAREVNA ...	118
THE TWO SONS OF IVAN THE SOLDIER	127
THE WOMAN-ACCUSER ..	143
THOMAS BERENNIKOV ...	150
THE WHITE DUCK	159
THE TALE OF LITTLE FOOL IVAN	165

	PAGE
THE LITTLE FEATHER OF FENIST THE BRIGHT FALCON	188
THE TALE OF THE PEASANT DEMYAN	200
THE ENCHANTED RING	201
THE BRAVE LABOURER	220
THE SAGE DAMSEL	222
THE PROPHETIC DREAM	229
TWO OUT OF THE KNAPSACK ...	245
THE STORY OF MARKO THE RICH AND VASILY THE LUCKLESS	252

LIST OF ILLUSTRATIONS.

THE GOLDEN MOUNTAIN	*Frontispiece.*	
MOROSKO	*To face page*	9
TSAREVNA LOVELINESS INEXHAUSTIBLE	,,	103
THE PRINCESS AND THE CUNNING WITCH ...	,,	160
THE DAMSEL WENT ON FURTHER, AND THE ROAD GREW LIGHTER AND LIGHTER ...	,,	198
THE SAGE DAMSEL ...	,,	224

RUSSIAN FAIRY TALES.

THE GOLDEN MOUNTAIN.

There was once upon a time a merchant's son who squandered and wasted all his goods. To such a pass did he come at last that he had nothing to eat. So he seized a spade, went out into the market-place, and began waiting to see if any one would hire him as a labourer. And behold, the merchant who was one in seven hundred[1] came along that way in his gilded coach; all the day-labourers saw him, and the whole lot of them immediately scattered in every direction and hid themselves in corners. The merchant's son alone of them all remained standing in the market-place. "Do you want work, young man?" said the merchant who was one in seven hundred; "then take

---

[1] *I. e.* the merchant who was seven hundred times richer than any one else.

RUSSIAN FAIRY TALES.

THE GOLDEN MOUNTAIN.

THERE was once upon a time a merchant's son who squandered and wasted all his goods. To such a pass did he come at last that he had nothing to eat. So he seized a spade, went out into the market-place, and began waiting to see if any one would hire him as a labourer. And behold, the merchant who was one in seven hundred[1] came along that way in his gilded coach; all the day-labourers saw him, and the whole lot of them immediately scattered in every direction and hid themselves in corners. The merchant's son alone of them all remained standing in the market-place. "Do you want work, young man?" said the merchant who was one in seven hundred; "then take

[1] *I. e.* the merchant who was seven hundred times richer than any one else.

hire from me."—"Right willingly; 'twas for no other reason that I came to the market-place."—"And what wage do you require?"—"If you lay me down one hundred roubles[1] a day, 'tis a bargain."—"That is somewhat dear!"—"If you think it dear, go and seek a cheaper article; but this I know, crowds of people were here just now, you came, and—away they all bolted."—"Well, agreed! come to-morrow to the haven." The next day, early in the morning, our merchant's son came to the haven; the merchant who was one in seven hundred had already been awaiting him some time. They went on board ship and went to sea. They sailed and sailed. In the midst of the sea an island appeared; on this island stood high mountains, and on the sea-shore something or other was burning like fire. "Can that which I see be fire?" said the merchant's son. "Nay, that is my little golden castle." They drew near to the island; they went ashore; his wife and daughter came forth to meet the merchant who was one in seven hundred, and the daughter was beautiful with a beauty that no man can imagine or devise, and no tale can tell. As soon as they had greeted one another they went on to the castle, and took the new labourer along with them; they sat them down at table, they began to eat, drink, and be merry. "A fig for to-day," said the host;

[1] 1 rouble = about 3*s*. 4*d*.

"to-day we'll feast, to-morrow we'll work." And the merchant's son was a fair youth, strong and stately, of a ruddy countenance like milk and blood, and he fell in love with the lovely damsel. She went out into the next room; she called him secretly, and gave him a flint and steel. "Take them," said she, "and if you should be in any need, use them." Next day the merchant who was one in seven hundred set out with his servant for the high golden mountain. They climbed and climbed, but they climbed not up to the top; they crawled and crawled, but they crawled not up to the top. "Well," said the merchant, "let's have a drink first of all." And the merchant handed him a sleeping poison. The labourer drank and fell asleep. The merchant drew out his knife, killed his wretched nag which he had brought with him, took out its entrails, put the young man into the horse's stomach, put the spade in too, sewed up the wound, and went and hid himself among the bushes. Suddenly there flew down a whole host of black iron-beaked ravens. They took up the carcase, carried it up into the mountain, and fell a-pecking it; they began eating up the horse, and soon pierced right down to the merchant's son. Then he awoke, beat off the black crows, looked hither and thither, and asked himself, "Where am I?" The merchant who was one in seven hundred bawled up at him, "On the golden mountain; come, take your spade and dig gold." So he digged and digged, throwing it all down below, and the merchant put it on wagons. By evening he had filled nine wagons. "That'll do," cried the merchant who was one in seven hundred; "thanks for your labour. Adieu!"—"But how about me?"—"You may get on as best you can. Ninety-nine of your sort have perished on that mountain—you will just make up the hundred!" Thus spake the merchant and departed. "What's to be done now?" thought the merchant's son; "to get down from this mountain is quite impossible. I shall certainly starve to death." So there he stood on the mountain, and above him wheeled the black iron-beaked crows, they plainly scented their prey. He began to bethink him how all this had come to pass, and then it occurred to him how the lovely damsel had taken him aside and given him the flint and steel, and said to him herself—"Take it, and if you are in need make use of it."—"And look now, she did not say it in vain. Let us try it." The merchant's son took out the flint and steel, struck it once, and immediately out jumped two fair young heroes. "What do you want? What do you want?"—"Take me from this mountain to the sea-shore." He had no sooner spoken than they took him under the arms and bore him carefully down from the mountain. The merchant's son walked about

by the shore, and lo, a ship was sailing by the island.
"Hi, good ship-folk, take me with you!"—"Nay,
brother, we cannot stop, such a stoppage would lose
us one hundred knots." The mariners passed by
the island, contrary winds began to blow, a frightful
hurricane arose. "Alas! he is plainly no simple man
of our sort, we had better turn back and take him on
board ship." So they returned to the island, stopped
by the shore, took up the merchant's son, and conveyed him to his native town. A long time and a
little time passed by, and then the merchant's son
took his spade and again went out into the marketplace to wait for some one to hire him. Again the
merchant who was one in seven hundred passed by
in his gilded carriage; the day-labourers saw him and
scattered in every direction, and hid them in corners.
The merchant's son was the sole solitary little one
left. "Will you take hire from me?" said the merchant who was one in seven hundred. "Willingly;
put down two hundred roubles a day, and set me my
work."—"Rather dear, eh?"—"If you find it dear, go
and seek cheaper labour. You saw how many people
were here, and the moment you appeared they all ran
away."—"Well, then, done; come to-morrow to the
haven." The next morning they met at the haven,
went on board the ship, and sailed to the island.
There they ate and drank their fill one whole day,

and the next day they got up and went towards the golden mountain. They arrived there, the merchant who was one in seven hundred pulled out his drinking-glass. "Come now, let us have a drink first," said he.—"Stop, mine host! You who are the chief ought to drink the first, let me treat you with mine own drink." And the merchant's son, who had betimes provided himself with sleeping poison, poured out a full glass of it and gave it to the merchant who was one in seven hundred. He drank it off and fell into a sound sleep. The merchant's son slaughtered the sorriest horse, disembowelled it, laid his host in the horse's belly, put the spade there too, sewed up the wound, and went and hid himself among the bushes. Instantly the black iron-beaked crows flew down, took up the carcase, carried it to the mountain, and fell a-pecking at it. The merchant who was one in seven hundred awoke and looked hither and thither. "Where am I?" he asked. "On the mountain," bawled the merchant's son. "Take your spade and dig gold; if you dig much, I will show you how to get off the mountain." The merchant who was one in seven hundred took his spade and dug and dug, he dug up twenty wagon loads. "Stop, that's enough now," said the merchant's son; "thanks for your labour, and good-bye."—"But what about me?"—"You? why, get off as best you can. Ninety-nine of your sort have perished on that mountain, you can make up the hundred." So the merchant's son took all the twenty wagons, went to the golden castle, married the lovely damsel, the daughter of the merchant who was one in seven hundred, took possession of all her riches, and came to live in the capital with his whole family. But the merchant who was one in seven hundred remained there on the mountain, and the black iron-beaked crows picked his bones.

MOROZKO.[1]

THERE was once a stepmother who, besides her stepdaughter, had a daughter of her own. Whatever her own daughter might do, she looked kindly at her and said, "Sensible darling!" but as for the stepdaughter, whatever she might do to please, it was always taken amiss. Everything she did was wrong, and not as it should be. Yet, sooth to say, the little stepdaughter was as good as gold; in good hands she would have swum in cheese and butter, but, living with her stepmother, she bathed herself every day in tears. What was she to do? The blast, though it blows, does not blow for ever, but a scolding old woman it is not so easy to avoid. She will take anything into her head, even to combing one's teeth. And the stepmother took it into her head to drive her stepdaughter from the house. "Take her, take

[1] Caressing diminutive of Russian *moroz* (frost). Perhaps "Jack Frost" is the nearest English equivalent.

her away, my old man, whithersoever you like, that mine eyes may not see her, that my ears may not hear of her; but don't take her to my own daughter in the warm room, but take her into the bare fields to the bitter, biting frost." The old man began to lament and weep, but for all that he put his daughter in the sledge; he would have liked to cover her with the horse-cloth, but even that he dared not do. So he took the homeless one into the bare fields, threw her on a heap of snow, crossed himself, and hastened home as fast as possible, that his eyes might not see his daughter's death.

There the poor little thing remained on the fringe of the forest, sat down under a fir-tree, shivered, and softly said her prayers. All at once she heard something. Morozko was crackling in a fir-tree not far off, and he leaped from fir to fir and snapped his fingers. And look! now he has come to that fir beneath which the girl was sitting; and he snapped his fingers, and leaped up and down, and looked at the pretty girl. "Maiden, maiden, 'tis I—Moroz-ruby-nose!"—"Welcome, Moroz! God must have sent thee to my poor sinful soul."—"Art thou warm, maiden?"—"Warm, warm, dear little father Moroz-ushko[1]!" Moroz began to descend lower, and crackle still more, and snap his fingers more than ever, and

[1] *I. e.* darling Moroz.

again he began speaking to the girl. "Art thou warm, maiden? Art thou warm, beauty?" The girl was scarce able to draw her breath, and yet she kept on saying, "Yes, warm, Morozushko; warm, little father!" Morozko crackled more than ever, and snapped his fingers harder and yet harder, and he said to the maiden for the last time, "Art thou warm, maiden? Art thou warm, beauty? Art thou warm, sweet clover?" The girl was all benumbed, and it was only in a voice scarcely audible that she could say, "Oh, yes! warm, darling little pigeon mine, Morozushko!" Morozko quite loved her for her pretty speeches. He had compassion on the girl; he wrapped her in furs, warmed her with warm coverings, and brought her a coffer, high and heavy, full of bridal garments, and gave her a robe all garnished with gold and silver. She put it on, and oh, how beautiful and stately she looked! And she sat down and began to sing songs. And the stepmother was preparing her funeral feast and frying pancakes. "Be off, husband, and bury your daughter!" she cried. And off the old man went. But the little dog under the table said, "Bow-wow! the old man's daughter is going about in silver and gold, but the old woman's daughter no wooers will look at."—"Silence, you fool! There's a pancake for you, and now say, 'The wooers will take the old woman's daughter, but there's

nothing left of the old man's daughter but her bones.'"
The little dog ate the pancake, but again he said,
"Bow-wow! the old man's daughter goes about in
silver and gold, but the old woman's daughter no
wooers will look at." The old woman kept beating
the dog and giving him pancakes, but the little dog
would have his way, and said, "The old man's
daughter goes about in silver and gold, but the old
woman's daughter no wooers will look at."

The floors creaked, the doors flew open wide, and
in they brought the high and heavy coffer, and behind
it walked the stepdaughter, in gold and silver, glittering like the sun. The stepmother looked at her, and
threw up her arms. "Old man, old man! put to
a pair of horses, and take my daughter at once. Put
her in the selfsame field, in the selfsame place." And
the old man took the daughter to the selfsame place.
And Moroz-ruby-nose came and looked at his guest,
and began to ask her, "Art thou warm, maiden?"—
"Be off with you!" replied the old woman's daughter,
"or are you blind not to see that my arms and legs are
quite benumbed with cold?" Morozko began skipping
and jumping, fair words were not to be expected from
that quarter. And he was angry with the stepdaughter, and froze her to death.

"Old man, old man! go and fetch my daughter.
Put to my swift horses, and don't overturn the sledge

and upset the coffer." But the little dog under the table said, "Bow-wow! the wooers will wed the old man's daughter, but they'll bring home nothing of the old woman's daughter but a sack of bones."—"Don't lie! There's a cake. Take it and say, 'They'll carry about the old woman's daughter in gold and silver!'" And the doors flew open, the nasty old woman ran out to meet her daughter, and instead of her she embraced a cold corpse. She began to howl and cry; she knew then that she had lost her wicked and envious daughter.

THE FLYING SHIP.

THERE was once upon a time an old man and an old woman, and they had three sons; two were clever, but the third was a fool. The old woman loved the first two, and quite spoiled them, but the latter was always hardly treated. They heard that a writing had come from the Tsar which said, "Whoever builds a ship that can fly, to him will I give my daughter the Tsarevna to wife." The elder brothers resolved to go and seek their fortune, and they begged a blessing of their parents. The mother got ready their things for the journey, and gave them something to eat on the way, and a flask of wine. And the fool began to beg them to send him off too. His mother told him he should not go. "Whither would you go, fool?" said she; "why, the wolves would devour you!" But the fool was always singing the same refrain: "I will go, I will go!" His mother saw that she could do nothing with him, so she gave him a piece of dry bread and a flask of water, and quickly shoved him out of the house.

The fool went and went, and at last he met an old man. They greeted each other. The old man asked the fool, " Whither are you going?"—" Look now!" said the fool, " the Tsar has promised to give his daughter to him who shall make a flying ship!"—" And can you then make such a ship?"—" No, I cannot, but they'll make it for me somewhere."—" And where is that somewhere?"—" God only knows."—" Well, in that case, sit down here; rest and eat a bit. Take out what you have got in your knapsack."—" Nay, it is such stuff that I am ashamed to show it to people."—" Nonsense! Take it out! What God has given is quite good enough to be eaten." The fool undid his knapsack, and could scarcely believe his eyes—there, instead of the dry crust of bread, lay white rolls and divers savoury meats, and he gave of it to the old man. So they ate together, and the old man said to the fool, " Go into the wood, right up to the first tree, cross yourself thrice, and strike the tree with your axe, then fall with your face to the ground and wait till you are aroused. Then you will see before you a ship quite ready; sit in it and fly wherever you like, and gather up everything you meet on your road." So our fool blessed the old man, took leave of him, and went into the wood. He went up to the first tree and did exactly as he had been commanded; he crossed himself three times, struck the tree with his axe, fell with his face to the ground, and went to sleep. In a little while some one or other awoke him. The fool rose up, and saw the ship quite ready, and without thinking long about it, he sat in it, and the ship flew up into the air. It flew and flew, and look!—there on the road below, a man was lying with his ear to the damp earth. "Good-day, uncle!"—"Good-day."—"What are you doing?"—"I am listening to what is going on in the world."—"Take a seat in the ship beside me." The man did not like to refuse, so he sat in the ship, and they flew on further. They flew and flew, and look!—a man was coming along hopping on one leg, with the other leg tied tightly to his ear. "Good-day, uncle; what are you hopping on one leg for?"—"Why, if I were to untie the other I should stride half round the world at a single stride."—"Come and sit with us." The man sat down, and they flew on. They flew and flew, and look!—a man was standing with a gun and taking aim, but at what they could not see. "Good-day, uncle; at what are you aiming? Not even a bird is to be seen."—"What! I am shooting at short range. I could hit bird or beast at a distance of one hundred leagues. That's what I call shooting!"

—"Sit down with us." This man also sat with them, and they flew on further. They flew and flew, and look!—a man was carrying on his back a whole sack-load of bread. "Good-day, uncle; whither are you going?"—"I am going," he said, "to get some bread for dinner."—"But you've got a whole sackload on your back already!"—"That! Why I should think nothing of eating all that at a single mouthful."—"Come and sit with us." The Gobbler sat in the ship, and they went flying on further. They flew and they flew, and look!—a man was walking round a lake. "Good-day, uncle; what are you looking for?"—"I want to drink, but I can find no water."—"But there's a whole lake before you, why don't you drink of it?"—"That! Why that water would not be more than a mouthful to me!" —"Then come and sit with us." He sat down, and again they flew on. They flew and flew, and look!— a man was walking in the forest, and on his shoulders was a bundle of wood. "Good-day, uncle; why are you dragging about wood in the forest?"—"But this is not common wood."—"What sort is it then?"— "It is of such a sort that if you scatter it, a whole army will spring up."—"Sit down with us then." He sat down with them, and they flew on further. They flew and flew, and look!—a man was carrying a sack of straw. "Good-day, uncle; whither are you carrying that straw?"—"To the village."—"Is there little straw in the village then?"—"Nay, but this straw is of such a kind that if you scatter it on the hottest summer day, cold will immediately set in with snow and frost."—"Won't you sit with us, then?"—"Thank you, I will."

Soon they flew into the Tsar's courtyard. The Tsar was sitting at table just then; he saw the flying ship, was much surprised, and sent out his servant to ask who was flying on that ship. The servant went to the ship and looked, and brought back word to the Tsar that 'twas but a single, miserable little muzhik[1] who was flying the ship. The Tsar fell a-thinking. He did not relish the idea of giving his daughter to a simple muzhik, and began to consider how he could rid him of this wretched son-in-law for a whole year. And so he thought, "I'll give him many grievous tasks to do." So he immediately sent out to the fool with the command to get him, by the time the imperial meal was over, living and singing water. Now, at the very time when the Tsar was giving this command to his servant, the first comrade whom the fool had met (that is to say, the one who was listening to what was going on in the world) heard what the Tsar said, and told it to the fool. "What shall I do now?" said the

[1] A peasant.

fool. "Why, if I search for a year, and for my whole life too, I shall never find such water."—"Don't be afraid," said Swift-of-foot to him, "I'll manage it for you." The servant came and made known the Tsar's command. "Say I'll fetch it," replied the fool, and his comrade untied his other leg from his ear, ran off, and in a twinkling he drew from the end of the world some of the living and singing water. "I must make haste and return presently," said he, and he sat down under a water-mill and went to sleep. The Tsar's dinner was drawing to a close, and still he did not turn up though they were all waiting, so that those on board the ship grew uneasy. The first comrade bent down to the earth and listened. "Oh ho! so you are asleep beneath the mill, are you?" Then the marksman seized his gun, shot into the mill, and awoke Swift-of-foot with his shooting. Swift-of-foot set off running, and in a moment he had brought the water. The Tsar had not yet risen from the table, and his command could not therefore have been more exactly fulfilled. But it was all to no purpose, another task had to be imposed. The Tsar bade them say to the fool, "Come now, as you are so smart, show what you're made of! You and your comrades must eat at one meal twenty roast oxen and twenty large measures of baked bread." The first comrade heard and told

this to the fool. The fool was terrified, and said,
"Why, I can't eat even one whole loaf at one meal!"
—"Don't be afraid," said Gobbler, "that will be very
little for me." The servant came and delivered the
Tsar's command. "Good!" said the fool, "let us
have it and we'll eat it." And they brought twenty
roasted bullocks, and twenty measures of baked
bread. Gobbler alone ate it all up. "Ugh!" he said,
"precious little! they might have given us a little
more." The Tsar bade them say to the fool that
he must now drink forty barrels of wine, each barrel
holding forty buckets. The first comrade of the
fool heard these words, and told them to him beforehand.
The fool was horrified. "Why, I could not
drink a single bucketful," said he. "Don't be
frightened," said the Drinker, "I'll drink for all;
it will be little enough for me." They poured out
the forty barrels of wine; the Drinker came and
drank the whole lot at one draught; he drank it
right to the dregs, and said, "Ugh! little enough,
too! I should have liked as much again." After
that the Tsar commanded the fool to get ready for
his wedding, and go to the bath-room to have a
good wash. Now this bath-room was of cast-iron,
and the Tsar commanded that it should be heated
hotter than hot, that the fool might be suffocated
therein in a single instant. So they heated the

bath red-hot. The fool went to wash himself, and behind him came the muzhik with the straw. "I must straw the floor," said he. They locked them both in the bath-room; the muzhik scattered the straw, and it became so cold that the fool was scarce able to wash himself properly, the water in the bath froze so hard. He crept up on the stove and there he passed the whole night. In the morning they opened the bath, and they found the fool alive and well, lying on the stove and singing songs. They brought word thereof to the Tsar. The Tsar was sore troubled, he did not know how to rid himself of the fool. He thought and thought, and commanded him to produce a whole army of his own devising. "How will a simple muzhik be able to form an army?" thought he; "he will certainly not be able to do that." As soon as the fool heard of this he was much alarmed. "Now I am quite lost," said he; "you have delivered me from my straits more than once, my friends, but it is plain that nothing can be done now."

"You're a pretty fellow," said the man with the bundle of wood; "why, you've clean forgotten me, haven't you?" The servant came and told the fool the Tsar's command: "If you will have the Tsarevna to wife, you must put on foot a whole army by morning."

"Agreed. But if the Tsar, even after this, should refuse, I will conquer his whole Tsardom and take the Tsarevna by force." At night the fool's companion went out into the fields, took his bundle of wood, and began scattering the faggots in different directions—and immediately a countless army appeared, both horse and foot. In the morning the Tsar saw it, and was terrified in his turn, and in all haste he sent to the fool precious ornaments and raiment, and bade them lead him to court and marry him to the Tsarevna. The fool attired himself in these costly ornaments, and they made him look handsomer than words can tell. He appeared before the Tsar, wedded the Tsarevna, received a large wedding-gift, and became quite clever and witty. The Tsar and the Tsaritsa[1] grew very fond of him, and the Tsarevna lived with him all her life, and loved him as the apple of her eye.

[1] The consort of the Tsar.

THE MUZHICHEK[1]-AS-BIG-AS-YOUR-THUMB-WITH-MOUSTACHES-SEVEN-VERSTS[2]-LONG.

In a certain kingdom, in a certain empire, there once lived a Tsar. At his royal court there was a harness of golden rings. Now it fell out that this Tsar once dreamed that in this harness was fastened a strange horse, not woolly white, but silvery bright, and on its brow a glistening moon. On awaking in the morning the Tsar commanded the public crier to cry abroad that whoever would interpret this dream, and discover this horse, should have his daughter in exchange, and half his tsardom into the bargain. At this royal proclamation a multitude of princes, boyards,[3] and great lords came together, and thought and thought, but not one of them could interpret the dream, not one of them could discover the horse. At last they hunted up a little withered old grey-beard

---

[1] *Lit.* little peasant; but here, gnome or goblin.
[2] A verst = 3500 English feet.   [3] Magnates.

Muzhichek,[1] and he said to the Tsar, "Thy dream was not a dream, but real. On just such a horse as thou didst see in thy dream, there came to thee in the night the Muzhichek-as-big-as-your-thumb-with-moustaches-seven-versts-long, and he wants to steal away your lovely little daughter out of the strong fortress."—"I thank thee, good man, for thy interpretation; and now wilt thou not tell me who can get me this horse?"—"I will tell thee, my Lord Tsar. I have three sons, mighty men of valour. My wife bore me all three of them in a single night; the eldest in the evening, the second at midnight, the third at dawn of day, and so we called them Zor'ka,[2] Vechorka,[3] and Polunochka.[4] They have not their equals in this realm for strength or valour. Look now, my little father and sovereign lord, send them forth that they may seek this strange horse for thee."—"Let them go, dear old friend. Let them take as much from my treasury as they need, nor will I go back from my royal word; whichever of them brings me this horse, to him will I give the Tsarevna and half my tsardom."

The next day, early in the morning, the three

[1] Little peasant.
[2] Diminutive of *Zorya*, the Red Dawn.
[3] Diminutive of *Vecher*, Evening.
[4] Diminutive of *Polunoch*, Midnight.

brother-heroes, Zor'ka, Vechorka, and Polunochka, arrived at the Tsar's court; the first had the fairest face, the second the broadest shoulders, the third the stateliest figure. They went in to the Tsar, prayed before the sacred ikons, and bowed low on every side of them, but to the Tsar they bowed lowest of all. "May our Sovereign Lord and Tsar live long in the land! We have come to thee, not to feast with the festive, but to do a deed right hard and sore, for we have come to fetch thee this strange horse from far away—that selfsame horse that appeared to thee in thy dreams."—"Success attend you, ye good youths! What provision do ye require for your journey?"—"We want nothing, O Gosudar![1] Only do not neglect our good father and mother. Provide for them in their old age and need."—"If that be all, depart in God's name on your journey. I will bring your old parents to my court, and they shall be my guests; I will give them to eat and drink from my own royal table, they shall be clothed and shod from my own royal wardrobe, and they shall be filled full with all good things."

So the good youths departed on their long journey. They travelled that day, and the next, and the third also, with nothing but the sky above their heads, and the broad steppe on every side of them. At last

[1] Emperor.

they left the steppe and entered a dense forest, and rejoiced greatly. On the very skirts of the forest stood a little hut, and beside the little hut a tiny sheepfold full of sheep. "Look," said they, "there we shall find some place to lay our heads in, and rest from our journey." They knocked at the hut—there was no answer; they peeped into it—it was quite empty. The brothers entered in, made ready for the night, prayed to God, and laid them down to sleep. In the morning Zor'ka and Polunochka went into the wood to hunt, and said to Vechorka, "Stay at home and get dinner ready for us." The eldest brother agreed, put everything to rights in the hut, and then went to the sheepfold, chose the fattest ram, cut it up, cleansed it, and roasted it for dinner. He had no sooner laid the table, however, and had just sat down by the window to await his brothers, when all at once there came a rumbling and a thundering from the forest, the door was nearly torn off its hinges, and the Muzhichek-only-as-big-as-your-thumb-but-with-moustaches-seven-versts-long entered the hut, with his moustaches floating far down his back. On entering the hut he looked at Vechorka from beneath his beetling brows, and shrieked with a terrible voice, "How dare you come into my hut as if you were its lord and master? How dare you cut up my ram?" But Vechorka looked at him and smiled. "You ought to grow a little bigger before you shriek like that," said he. "Be off, and don't let me see you here again, or I'll take a spoonful of cabbage soup, and a little crumb of bread, and glue up your eyes for you." The Muzhichek-no-bigger-than-your-thumb-but-with-moustaches-seven-versts-long replied, "I see that you don't know that, though small, I am brave withal;" then, tearing the hero from the bench, he dragged him from corner to corner, bumped his head well against the walls, and then threw him, more dead than alive, beneath the bench. He himself took the roast ram from the table, ate it, bones and all, and vanished. The brothers returned and asked, "What's the matter? Why have you bandaged your head?" But Vechorka was ashamed to say that such a miserable little wretch had trounced him so soundly, and he said to his brothers, "I got a headache from looking to the fire without you, so that I could neither roast nor boil."

The next day Zor'ka and Vechorka went out to hunt, and Polunochka stayed behind to get the dinner ready. No sooner had he finished cooking the dinner, than there was again a rushing sound in the wood, and into the hut came the Muzhichek-no-bigger-than-your-thumb-but-with-moustaches-seven-versts-long, knocked Polunochka about, maimed him, pitched him under the bench, ate up the whole dinner, and vanished. Again the brothers returned and asked, "What's the matter, brotherkin? Why do you tie up your head with rags?"—"I have got a headache from looking to the fire, my brothers," replied Polunochka, "so that my poor little head was quite splitting, and therefore I could not get ready your dinner for you."

On the third day the elder brothers went to hunt, and Zor'ka remained in the hut alone, and thought to himself, "There's something not quite right here. It is not for nothing that my brothers have complained of the heat of the fire two days running." So he began to look all about, and to listen, in case any one should be coming to fall upon him unawares. He chose a ram, killed and cut it up, cleansed it, roasted it, and placed it on the table, and immediately there was a racket and a thundering in the wood, and in at the door rushed the Muzhichek-no-bigger-than-your-thumb-but-with-moustaches-seven-versts-long, with a rick of hay on his head, and in his hand a bucket of water. He put the bucket of water in the midst of the courtyard, strewed the straw all over the courtyard, and set about counting his sheep. He saw that there was yet another ram missing, flew into a violent rage, stamped on the ground with his little feet, dashed into the hut, and flung himself violently upon Zor'ka. But this Zor'ka was not like his brothers. He seized the Muzhichek by his moustaches, and began to drag him about the hut and well towzle him, and cried at the same time—

> "If you don't know the ford
> Don't step overboard."[1]

The Muzhichek-no-bigger-than-your-thumb wriggled about from side to side, tore himself out of Zor'ka's iron paws, though he left the ends of his moustaches in his fists, and ran away from him as hard as he could, Zor'ka after him—but whither, pray? He flew up into the air like fluff, vanished from before his eyes, and was gone. Zor'ka returned to the hut, and sat down by the window to await his beloved brothers. The brothers arrived, and were quite astonished to find him hale and whole, and the dinner ready. But Zor'ka drew out from his girdle the ends of the long moustaches which he had torn from the monster, and said to his brothers, with a smile, "Look, my brothers, I have twisted your headache that you caught from the fire[2] round my girdle! I see now that neither in strength nor stout-heartedness are ye fit comrades for me, so I will go on alone to discover the wondrous steed, but you go back to the village and plough land." Then he took leave of his brothers, and went on his way.

[1] *I. e.* caution's the best policy.
[2] *Ugar*, lit. the suffocating fire-smoke.

Just as he was leaving the wood, Zor'ka came upon a crazy little hut, and in this crazy little hut he heard some one crying dolorously, "Whoever will give me to eat and to drink, him will I serve." The good youth went into the hut, and saw that on the stove lay an armless, legless one, piteously groaning, and begging for meat and drink. Zor'ka gave him to eat and drink, and asked him who he was. "A hero was I, no whit worse than thou, but lo! I ate one of the rams of the Muzhichek-no-bigger-than-your-thumb, and he made me a cripple for the rest of my life. But because you have had compassion upon me, and given me both to eat and to drink, I will show you how to get the wondrous horse."—"Show me, I pray, good man."—"Go, then, to the river hard by, take a ferry-boat on it, ferry people across it the whole year round, take money from none, and—you'll see what will happen."

Zor'ka went to the river, took a ferry-boat, and a whole year round he ferried everybody across gratis. And it befell him once that he had to ferry over three old pilgrims. The old men got out on the bank, and began to undo their travelling purses, and the first pulled out a whole handful of gold, the second a whole roll of pure pearls, and the third the most precious stones. "There, that is for thy ferrying, good youth," said the old men. "I can take nothing from you," said Zor'ka, "because I am here, according to promise, to ferry every one across without taking money for it."—"Then for what dost thou do it?"—"I seek the wondrous horse which is not woolly white, but silvery bright, and I can find it nowhere; so that is why good people have advised me to hire a ferry-boat here, and they said, you shall see what will happen."—"Well for thee, good youth, that thou hast been true to thy word; we can equip thee for thy journey. Here is a little ring for thy little finger, do but transfer it from finger to finger, and all thy wishes will be gratified." And the old men went on their way, but Zor'ka immediately put the ring on the other hand and said—"Let me be at once in those places where the Muzhichek-no-bigger-than-your-thumb lives and pastures his horse!" And immediately the tempest took him, and before he could wink once he found himself in front of a deep chasm amongst the gloomy rocks, and he saw that in this side of the chasm, but on the very edge of it, was sitting the Muzhichek-no-bigger-than-your-thumb-but-with-moustaches-seven-versts-long, and around him was pacing the wondrous horse that was not woolly white, but silvery bright; on its brow shone a moon, and many stars were in its mane. "Welcome, good youth!" screeched the monster to Zor'ka; "what brings you hither?"—"I am going to take your horse away from you."—"Nay, 'tis not for you nor for any one else to take him from me. If I but seize him by the mane and lead him to the edge of this abyss, nobody in the world can take him away from hence, though they strive for ever and ever."—"Well, then, let us exchange."—"Willingly. I don't mind exchanging with you. You bring me hither the daughter of your Tsar, and I will give you my horse, and you may lead him from field to field."—"Good," said Zor'ka, and he immediately began considering how he might get the better of the monster. He transferred his ring from finger to finger, and said, "Let the lovely Tsarevna immediately appear here before me." And in the twinkling of an eye the Tsarevna appeared before him, all pale and trembling, and fell down on her knees before him, and begged and prayed him: "Good youth, wherefore hast thou conjured me away from my father? Oh, spare my tender youth!" But Zor'ka whispered her, "I want to get the better of that monster there. I'll make believe to exchange you for the horse, and leave you with the monster as his wife; but you take this ring, and when you want to return home you have only to take it off one finger and put it on the other, and say, 'I want to turn into a little needle to stick it into Zor'ka behind his collar,' and you'll see what will happen." And as Zor'ka had said to the Tsarevna, so it fell out. He gave the Tsarevna to the monster in exchange for the wondrous horse, put his martial harness on the horse, mounted, and went on his way; but the Muzhichek-no-bigger-than-your-thumb laughed and shouted after him, " 'Tis well, good youth; thou hast exchanged a lovely damsel for a horse." Zor'ka had not gone two or three versts when he felt something pricking him behind the collar. He put his hand there, and lo! there was a needle. He pitched it on the ground, and before him stood a lovely damsel, who wept and begged him to take her back to her dear father's house. Zor'ka set her on the horse beside him, and galloped off as only heroes can gallop. He arrived at the Tsar's court, and found the Tsar in an evil mood. The Tsar said to him, "I rejoice not at all, good youth, in thy faithful service, nor do I require the steed thou hast gotten for me, nor will I reward thee with aught according to thy merits."—"And wherefore, pray, dear father Tsar?"—"Because, good youth, my daughter went away without my leave."—"Nay, but, my Sovereign Lord and Tsar, it beseems thee not to trifle with me so: the Tsarevna was only this instant greeting me from out of her stronghold." Then the Tsar rushed into the stronghold, where he still found his daughter, embraced her, and brought her out to the good youth. "Here is thy reward and my delight." And the Tsar took the horse, and gave his daughter to Zor'ka to wife, and half his tsardom along with her into the bargain. And Zor'ka still lives with his wife, and cannot love her enough, and he rejoices in his good fortune without over-much boasting.

THE STORY OF THE TSAREVICH IVAN, AND OF THE HARP THAT HARPED WITHOUT A HARPER.

FAR, far behind the blue sea, behind the fiery abyss, in the void places, in the midst of the pleasant meadows, stood a lofty city, and in this city ruled Tsar Umnaya Golova[1] with his Tsaritsa. There they lived a long time, and to their great delight a daughter was born to them, a most lovely Tsarevna whom they called Neotsyenaya,[2] and the next year there was born to them another daughter just as lovely, and her they named the Tsarevna Beztsyenaya.[3] In his joy Tsar Umnaya Golova made merry and gladdened his heart, and feasted and ate and drank to his heart's content. He gave his voevods[4] three hundred and three buckets of mead to toast him in, and bade them regale his whole realm with beer for three

[1] Wise Head.   [2] Not to be priced.
[3] Without price.   [4] Generals and high officials.

days. Whoever liked might drink, and good measure was meted out to him. Now, when all the feastings and junketings were over, Tsar Umnaya Golova began to be troubled with the thought how to feed and nourish and train up his beloved daughters, and bring them under the golden crown.[1] Great were the cares of the Tsar concerning his daughters. They were only fed with gold spoons, they were laid to sleep on eider-down beds, they were covered with sable coverlets, and three nurses took it in turn to drive away the flies when the Tsarevnas laid them down to sleep. Tsar Umnaya Golova bade them watch over his daughters, and take care that the lovely sun never looked into their room with his bright rays, that the cold dew never fell on them, and that the truant wind never dared to blow upon them. And for the defence and protection of his daughters, the Tsar placed beside them seventy-seven nurses, and seventy-seven guardians—a certain wise man advised him to do so.

Thus Tsar Umnaya Golova with his Tsaritsa and his two daughters lived and thrived together. I know not how many years passed by, and the Tsarevnas began to grow up, fill out, and become beautiful. Wooers already began to make their appearance at the Tsar's court, but Tsar Umnaya

[1] Crowns are put on the heads of Greek brides.

Golova was in no great haste to marry off his daughters. He reflected that a destined wooer cannot be avoided even on a swift horse, while a wooer that is not destined cannot be held fast by triple iron chains, and while he was thus thinking and casting the matter over in his mind, he suddenly heard a great noise and commotion. There was a scampering up and down and to and fro in his courtyard. The outdoor nurses were crying, the indoor nurses were howling, and the guardians were bawling with all their might. Tsar Umnaya Golova immediately rushed out and asked, "What is the matter?" Then the seventy-seven male attendants, and the seventy-seven female attendants all fell down on their knees before him. "We are guilty," they cried; "look now! the Tsarevnas Neotsyenaya and Beztsyenaya have been carried off by a whirlwind!" A strange thing had happened. The Tsarevnas had gone out to walk in the Tsar's garden to pluck a few sweet-peas and wrench off a red poppy or two, and feast upon a few ripe pippins. Suddenly a black cloud rose up above them (whence it came nobody knew), blew right into the eyes of the nurses and guardians, and by the time they had come to themselves and begun to rub their eyes, all trace of the Tsarevnas had vanished, there was nothing for the eye to see or the ear to hear. Tsar Umnaya Golova regularly flared up with rage. "I will deliver you all over to an evil death!" said he. "You shall perish miserably in dungeons; I will bid them shoot at you with peas in the gates. What! seven-and-seventy of you nurses, and seven-and-seventy of you guardians, could not look after two Tsarevnas!"

And now Tsar Umnaya Golova was in sore trouble and affliction; he neither ate, nor drank, nor slept; everything was a grief and a burden to him; banquets at his court there were none, and the sound of the fiddle and the shawm was heard there no more. Only sad grief sat beside him and sang her mournful dirge like the croaking of a crow of evil omen.

But time passes and sorrow with it. The life of man is like a variegated tapestry, interwoven with dark flowers and bright. Time moved onwards, and then another child was born to the Tsar, but this time it was not a Tsarevna, but a Tsarevich. Tsar Umnaya Golova rejoiced greatly; he called his son Ivan, and placed beside him old-men nurses, foster-fathers, wise teachers, and valiant voevods. And the Tsarevich Ivan began to grow and grow just as wheaten meal swells and swells when good yeast is put to it. He grew not by the day but by the hour, and what wondrous beauty, what a stately figure was his! One thing only weighed upon the heart of Tsar Umnaya Golova: good and beauteous was the Tsarevich Ivan, but there was nothing in him of heroic valour or of knightly skill. He did not tear off the heads of his comrades, nor break their arms and legs; he neither loved to play with lances of damask steel, nor with swords of tempered metal; he did not muster his strong battalions, nor hold converse with his voevods. Good and beauteous was the Tsarevich Ivan; he amazed all men with his wit and wisdom, and his sole delight was to play on the harp that needed no harper. And the Tsarevich Ivan played so that all men forgot all else as they listened. The moment he placed his fingers on the strings they sang and played with such a wondrous voice that the very dumb wept for sympathy, and the very legless danced for joy. Beautiful songs they were, but they did not replenish the Tsar's treasure, nor defend the realm, nor smite the evil foe.

And one day Tsar Umnaya Golova bade them bring the Tsarevich Ivan before him, and thus he spake to him: "My beloved son, good art thou and beauteous, and I am well content with thee. One thing only grieves me. I do not see in thee the valour of a warrior, or the skill of a champion. Thou dost not love the clash of steel lances and the tempered blade has no charm for thee. Look now! I am growing old, and we have savage foes. They will come to us, make our realm the spoil of war, put to death our boyars and voevods, and lead captive me and my Tsaritsa, for thou canst not defend us." The Tsarevich Ivan listened to the words of Tsar Umnaya Golova, and thus he made answer: "Dear Tsar-Gosudar and father! Not by strength but by craft are cities taken, not by cudgels but by cunning will I prevail against the foe. Make trial of my martial strength, make trial of my youthful valour. Look now! They tell me that I had two sisters, Tsarevnas, and that the truant whirlwind carried them away, and that the rumour of them vanished as if it were covered with snow. Call together now all thy princes, thy heroes, thy stalwart voevods, and bid them do thee the service of finding out my sisters, the Tsarevnas. Let them bring their damask blades, their iron lances, their glowing darts, and their countless soldiery; and if any one of them shall do thee this service, give to him my tsardom and bid me be unto him as a scullion, to lick his pots, and as a fool to make him sport. But if they cannot render thee this service, then I will render it thee, and then thou shalt see that my wisdom and my wit is sharper than a damask blade, and stronger than a lance of steel."

And the words of the Tsarevich pleased the Tsar. He called together his boyars, his voevods, his strong and mighty champions, and he said to them: "Is there any one of you, my boyars, voevods, strong and mighty champions, hero enough to go seek my daughters? If so, to him will I give to choose which of my daughters he will to be his love, and with her he shall have half my tsardom." The boyars, the voevods, and the champions looked one upon another, and hid one behind the other, but not one of them dared to speak. Then the Tsarevich Ivan bowed low before his father and said—"Dear Father-Gosudar! if none will take it upon him to render thee this paltry little service, give me thy blessing on my journey. I will go, I will seek my sisters, nor have I need of any royal gift from thee to enable me to do it."—"Good!" replied Tsar Umnaya Golova; "my blessing go with thee. Take also of my treasures, silver and gold and precious stones, and if thou requirest soldiers, take a hundred thousand horse and a hundred thousand foot also." And the Tsarevich Ivan replied, "I need neither silver nor gold, neither horse nor foot, neither the horse of the champion nor his sword and lance. I will take with me my sweet-sounding harp that plays of its own accord, and nothing else. And thou, my Sovereign Tsar, await me these three years, and if I come not again in the fourth year, then choose thee my successor." Then the Tsarevich Ivan received his father's blessing both in writing and by word of mouth, commended himself to God, took his harp under his arm, and went straight on his way whither his eyes led him. Whither was he to go to find his sisters? He went and went near and far, high and low. The tale of his going is soon told, but the deed that he did is not soon done. The Tsarevich Ivan went straight onwards, he went on and on, and as he went he played songs upon his harp; whenever the morning broke he arose again and wended his way along; when night fell he laid him down on the silky grass beneath the vast roof of the heavenly dome bright with stars. And at last he came to a dense forest. The Tsarevich Ivan heard a great cracking in this dense forest as if some one were smashing it, such a rumbling and a thundering was there in this forest. "What is this?" thought the Tsarevich Ivan; "a man must die once though no man can die twice." And his eyes filled with terror, for he saw two wood demons fighting. One was belabouring the other with an uprooted oak, and the other was pitching into his comrade with a pine tree five fathoms long, and the pair of them were fighting with all their devilish strength. The Tsarevich Ivan approached them with his harp and struck up a dance. The demons stopped short, began to dance some devilish dance, and kicked up their heels[1] with such vigour that the very welkin rang. They danced and they danced, they danced themselves off their legs and rolled on to the ground, and the Tsarevich Ivan began to talk to them. "Come now! what are you quarrelling for?" said he. "Ye, my children, are regular wood demons, and yet ye make fools of yourselves as if ye were common people." Then one of the wood demons said to him, "Wherefore should we not fight? Hearken and judge betwixt us! We were going on our way and we found something. I said, 'Tis mine; but he said, 'Tis mine—we tried to divide it and we could not divide it."—"And what then was it that you found?" asked the Tsarevich Ivan.—"This is what it was: a little bread-and-salt table-cloth, self-moving boots, and an invisible little cap. Dost thou want to eat and drink? Then spread out the little table-cloth, and twelve youths and twelve maids will bring thee mead to drink and sweetmeats as much as thou wilt! And if any one come that way, thou hast only to slip on the self-walking boots and thou canst go seven versts at one stride; nay, thou canst go even quicker than fourteen versts at one stride, so that no bird can fly level with thee and no wind can overtake thee. But if some unavoidable

[1] *Lit.* gave themselves up to a trepak. A trepak is a peculiarly wild popular dance.

calamity threaten thee thou hast but to put on thy little invisible cap, and thou vanishest so completely that the very dogs cannot scent out thy whereabouts."—"What a thing to quarrel about! Will ye agree to what I say if I divide what ye have found?" The wood demons agreed, and the Tsarevich Ivan said, "Look now! Run towards that little path, and whichever of you reaches it, he shall have the table-cloth, the boots, and the cap."—"Ah, now!" cried the wood demons, "that is common sense! Do thou hold the treasures and we will do the running." So away they went at full tilt, till nothing but their heels were visible and they disappeared in the forest. But the Tsarevich Ivan did not wait for them, he put the boots on his feet, the cap on his head, the little table-cloth under his arm, and made himself scarce as they call it. The wood demons came running back, but could not find the place where the Tsarevich had stood; but Ivan the Tsarevich, striding with great strides, got out of the wood and saw the wood demons running round him and beyond him, and trying to scent him out, but they could find nothing, and fell to wringing their hands.

Ivan the Tsarevich went on his way; he went on and on, he strode and strode, and he came to the open plains. Three roads lay before him, and in the cross-way stood a wretched little hut turning round and round on hen's legs. And Ivan the Tsarevich said to it, "Izbushka! izbushka!¹ turn your back to the wood and your front to me!" Then Ivan the Tsarevich stepped into the hut, and there in the hut was sitting Baba-Yaga² bony-leg. "Fie! fie! fie!" said Baba-Yaga, "up to this day a Russian soul has been a sight unknown to my eyes and a sound unknown to my ears, and now a Russian soul appears before my very eyes! For what hast thou come, good youth?"—"Oh, thou senseless Granny!" said the Tsarevich Ivan to her, "thou shouldst feed me well first, and only after that shouldst thou begin to ask questions." Baba-Yaga leaped up in the twinkling of an eye, heated her little stove, fed Ivan the Tsarevich, and then began to ask him, "Whither dost thou go, good youth, and whither does thy way lie?"—"I go," said Ivan the Tsarevich, "to seek my sisters, the Tsarevna Neotsyenaya and the Tsarevna Beztsyenaya. But now, dear little Granny, tell me, if thou knowest, what way must I go, and where shall I find them?"—"I know where the Tsarevna Neotsyenaya lives!" said Baba-Yaga; "thou must take the middle road to get to her, but she lives in the white stone palace of

---

¹ Wretched little hut.
² The witch of witches in Russian fairy tales.

her old husband the Forest Monster. The road thither is hard, far must thou go; and if thou gettest there 'twill boot thee little, for the Forest Monster will devour thee."—"Well, little Granny, perhaps it will choke him. A Russian man is a bony morsel, and God will not give him over to be eaten by a swine like that! Farewell! and thank you for your bread and salt!" And so the Tsarevich Ivan strode away from her, and look!—there, right across the plain, shone white and dazzling the stony palace of the Forest Monster. Ivan went up to it and saw the gate, and on the gate sat a sort of little devil who said, "No admittance!"—"Open, my friend!" replied Ivan the Tsarevich, "and I'll give thee some vodka!"[1] The little devil took the vodka, but he didn't open the gate for all that. Then Ivan the Tsarevich went round about the palace and resolved to climb over the wall. He climbed up and along and never observed the trap into which he was falling, for on the top of the walls wires were spread all about, and the moment the Tsarevich Ivan touched one of these wires with his foot all the bells fell a-ringing. Ivan the Tsarevich looked, and out upon the balcony rushed his sister the Tsarevna Neotsyenaya and said, "Is it thou then that hast come, my beloved brother, Ivan the Tsarevich?" And the

---

[1] Russian brandy.

brother and the sister embraced and kissed each other. "Where shall I hide thee from the Monster of the Forest?" said the Tsarevna Neotsyenaya, "for I believe he will be here at once."—"Where indeed, for I am no needle." The brother and sister were still talking when suddenly there was the dull roar of a tempest and whirlwind, all the palace trembled, and the Monster of the Forest appeared; but Ivan the Tsarevich put on his little invisible cap and became invisible. And the Forest Monster said, "Where then is thy guest who climbed over the wall?"—"I have no guest here at all," replied the Tsarevna Neotsyenaya, " but perhaps the sparrows have been flying over it and stuck to it with their wings!"—"Sparrows indeed! Methinks I smell the smell of a Russian soul here!"—"What are you dreaming about? You run about the wide world and do nothing but harass souls, and now you would vex other souls also!"—"Don't be angry, Tsarevna Neotsyenaya, I do no harm to thy happiness, only I have now a desire to eat, and I should like to eat up this unknown," said the Forest Monster. Ivan the Tsarevich, however, took off his invisible cap, bowed to the Forest Monster, and said, "Why do you want to eat me? Don't you see what a lean and bony morsel I am! Rather let me regale you with a breakfast such as you have never eaten since the day of your birth, only take care that you don't swallow your tongue and all!" Then Ivan the Tsarevich spread out his little bread-and-salt table-cloth, the twelve youths and the twelve damsels appeared, and began to regale the Forest Monster with as much as ever he could eat. The Forest Monster ate and ate and ate, then he drank, and then he ate again, till he was unable to stir from the spot; he fell asleep in the very place where he sat. "And now farewell, my beloved sister!" said the Tsarevich Ivan; "yet tell me, dost thou not know the place where our sister the Tsarevna Beztsyenaya dwells?"—"I know it," replied the Tsarevna Neotsyenaya; "thou must go to her along the great sea Ocean, there she dwells in the very whirlpool of the ocean with her old husband the Sea Monster; but the way thither is hard. Far, very far must thou swim, and if thou gettest there it will boot thee little, for he will devour thee!"— "Well," said the Tsarevich Ivan, "he may chew me perhaps, but he will find me a hard morsel to swallow. Farewell, sister!" And Ivan the Tsarevich began to stride onwards, and he came to the great sea Ocean. By the shore stood a boat such as the Russian people use when they go a-fishing; the shrouds and gear were of linden bast, the sails of fine hair mats, and the boat itself was not welded with nails, but sown fast with birch-bark. On this ship the mariners were getting ready to go to sea, to sail to the Rock-Salt Island. "Won't you take me with you?" said the Tsarevich Ivan; "I will pay you nothing for my passage, but I will tell you tales so that you will never notice how long the journey is." The ship-folk agreed, and they sailed away upon the great sea Ocean, they sailed past the Rock-Salt Island; the Tsarevich Ivan told them tales, and they sailed and sailed. Suddenly, whence they knew not, a tempest came flying up, the thunder began to growl, and the ship began to quake. "Alas!" shrieked the ship's folk, "to our own destruction have we listened to this fair speaker, never shall we see our dear little homes again, we shall descend into the whirlpools of Ocean! There is no help for it, we must pay tribute to the Monster of the Sea; let us cast lots, it will fall upon the guilty!" They cast lots, and it fell upon the Tsarevich Ivan. "It can't be helped, my brothers!" said the Tsarevich Ivan. "I thank you for your bread and salt; farewell, nor think amiss of me in time to come!" Then he took with him his self-walking boots, his little bread-and-salt table-cloth, his little invisible cap, and his harp that harped of its own accord, and they raised the good youth and swung him right out into the whirlpools of Ocean.

The sea became calm, the boat sped on, and the Tsarevich Ivan went like a key to the bottom, and stood upright on his legs in the halls of the Monster of the Sea, the wondrous flower-grown halls of ocean! The Sea Monster was sitting on his throne with the Tsarevna Beztsyenaya by his side, and the Sea Monster said, " 'Tis a long time since I have eaten fresh flesh, and lo! it comes right into my very hands! Welcome, friend! Come here, and let me see at which end of you I may begin!" Then the Tsarevich Ivan began to say that he was the brother of the Tsarevna Beztsyenaya, and that amongst good people one behaved not so badly as to eat another up. "That is too much!" shrieked the Sea Monster; "he comes to force his own rules and regulations upon the homes of other people!" Ivan the Tsarevich saw that things were going badly, so he took out his harp that played of its own accord, and when he began playing a plaintive air, the Sea Monster began to pull wry faces, then fell to sighing like a blacksmith's bellows, and wept and moaned just as if he had swallowed a needle; and then, when the Tsarevich Ivan struck up the air, "Let the merry churochki[1] go round the little table!" why then indeed the very halls put their arms akimbo and fell a-dancing, while the Sea Monster could not

[1] Small glass or bowl for drinking spirits.

skip up and down enough, but stamped with his feet, snapped with his fingers, rolled his eyes about, and pulled such faces that all the fishes flocked round to see, and nearly died for laughter. The Monster of the Sea thoroughly enjoyed himself. "Well!" said he, "'twould be a sin to eat such a youth. Stop here, stay with us, sit down and be our guest, won't you? Here are lots of herrings, pike, bream, and perch! Come, sit down at table, eat, drink, and be merry, my dear guest!" So Ivan the Tsarevich and the Tsarevna Beztsyenaya and the Sea Monster sat down, and ate and drank and made merry. A whale danced a German dance in front of them, the herrings sang glees, the carps performed on various instruments. After dinner the Sea Monster went to sleep, and the Tsarevna Beztsyenaya said, "My beloved brother, I am glad to see thee, dear guest; so far well, but 'twill not last for ever. When he awakes the Sea Monster will eat thee if the evil humour takes him."—"Tell me, darling sister," said the Tsarevich Ivan, "how I may save our sister Neotsyenaya from the Forest Monster, and thee from the Monster of the Sea?"—"If you like you may try your luck, but you'll find it, I think, a ticklish business. Behind the great sea Ocean here lies a large tsardom, and there reigns there not a Tsar, but a Tsaritsa called the Tsar-Maiden. If thou makest thy way thither, and gettest into her fenced garden, then the Tsar-Maiden will become thy consort, and she only can free us and restore us to our father and mother. But the mischief of it is this—she has a strict guard which will allow no one to cross the shore, a guard all bristling with guns and lances, and fastened to each lance is a head, and all these poor little heads are the heads of the youths who came to woo the Tsar-Maiden. There were tsars, tsareviches, kings, kings' sons, mightily strong warriors, and they came with hosts, and they sailed with ships, and were able to do nothing; all of them were stuck upon lances."—"Look now!" said the Tsarevich Ivan, "what is there to fear? Terrible are the threats of Heaven and manifold is the mercy of God. Tell me but how I may get to the tsardom of the Tsar-Maiden."—"But is it a wise thing to make thy way thither? Nevertheless I'll give thee my beloved sturgeon; sit upon him and go thy way, and my swift runner the long-nosed sterlet shall swim before thee to show the way." The brother and sister then said farewell, the Tsarevich Ivan sat him on the sturgeon and sped away, and the sterlet went on before to show the way. They fell in with some crabs, and they saluted the Tsarevich Ivan with their moustaches, and beat the drums with their clippers, and drove the little fishes out of the way. But the sea is not the same thing as the dry land. There was neither hemp nor bramble to hold on by, the way was slippery, as slippery as grease. The Tsarevich Ivan slipped and slipped. Then he put on his little invisible cap and saw that the guards of the Tsar-Maiden were opening wide their eyes and gazing afar off, and saw nothing that was going on beneath their noses, and they were still whetting their swords and sharpening their spears. And the Tsarevich Ivan came to the shore, the sturgeon set him safely on the quay, made an obeisance, and jumped into the water again; but the Tsarevich Ivan went past the guard without bending his knee, and entered the fenced garden as if he were the master there; he walked about, he walked all over it, he diverted himself, and ate of the luscious and transparent apples there.

And lo! the Tsarevich lingered and lingered there. And he saw twenty white doves flying towards a pond. They lighted on the ground and became twenty maidens lovely as the stars of heaven and as goodly as blood and milk. Amongst them the Tsar-Maiden was walking like a peacock, and said, "My beloved friends, 'tis hot; ye see how the sun burns like an oven. Let us bathe! No evil eye can see us here. So strong a guard stands on the shore that not even a fly could pass by them."—"A fly cannot pass them, eh! Look now what a big fly has passed them," said the Tsarevich Ivan, and he took off his little invisible cap and bowed low to the Tsar-Maiden. The Tsar-Maiden and her comrades, as maidens are wont to do, shrieked and moaned, thought of running away and didn't, made as though they wouldn't look and looked all the same, and winked and blinked with their eyes. "Tsar-Maiden, and ye, lovely damsels," said the Tsarevich Ivan, "wherefore do ye fear me? I am not a bear, I shall not bite you, I will take no one's heart against her will; but if my destined bride be here, then am I her destined bridegroom." Then the Tsar-Maiden turned as scarlet as the red poppy-flower, gave her white hand to the Tsarevich Ivan, and said, "Welcome, good youth! Whether thou be tsar or tsarevich, king or king's son, I know not; but if thou hast come hither as a gentle guest, thy reception shall be as beseemeth a dear friend. Many brutal wooers have come to me who would have taken my virginal heart by force, such a thing as was never heard of since the beginning of the world. Come into my white stone halls and into my crystal chambers!"

The whole nation heard that their Tsarevna, the Tsar-Maiden, had got her a bridegroom after her own heart, and they came in swarms both of young and old, and shouted and rejoiced with all their might. And the Tsar-Maiden commanded that the royal cellar should be opened for them, and that they should be allowed to beat drums and guitars and play fiddles; and the next day they played at the merry banquet and the wedding feast. And there were banquets for three days and rejoicings for three weeks. And after that the Tsarevich Ivan spoke to his consort about releasing his sisters, one from the Monster of the Forest and the other from the Monster of the Sea. "My beloved consort, Ivan the Tsarevich," she replied, "what would I not do for thee! Send and fetch me my hedgehog-lawyer and my sparrow-scribe, and let them send ukases to the Monster of the Forest and the Monster of the Sea, bidding them give up the sisters of Ivan the Tsarevich, or I will take them into custody and give them over to a cruel death." So the hedgehog-lawyer and the sparrow-scribe wrote out ukases and sent them off. And the Monster of the Forest and the Monster of the Sea could do nothing, so they set free the Tsarevna Neotsyenaya and the Tsarevna Beztsyenaya. And the Tsarevich Ivan wrote this letter to his father, the Tsar Umnaya Golova: "Thou seest, O Sovereign Tsar, that not with strength and valour only but with craft and wit also can one prevail over all.

And the self-playing harp is sometimes of as good service as the Damascus blade, although of course one must not lash it with a whip. And now come to me, dear father, and be my guest, and I will be with thee with my wife and my sisters. A goodly banquet is ready, and I wish thee long years and many." And so Ivan the Tsarevich lived a joyous life, and waxed rich and prosperous. And he lived long and reigned gloriously, and feasted me right royally, so I made up this merry tale about him.

THE STORY OF GORE-GORINSKOE.[1]

THERE once lived in a village two brothers, one of whom was rich, and the other poor. With the rich man everything went swimmingly, in everything he laid his hand to he found luck and bliss; but as for the poor man, slave and toil as he might, fortune flew away from him. The rich man, in a few years, so grew out of bounds that he went to live in the town, and built him the biggest house there, and settled down as a merchant; but the poor man got into such straits that sometimes he had not even a crust of bread in the house to feed a whole armful of children, small—smaller—smallest, who all cried together, and begged for something to eat and drink. And the poor man began to repine at his fate, he began to lose heart, and his dishevelled head began to sink deeper between his shoulders. And he went to his rich brother in the town and said, "Help me!

[1] *I.e.* Woeful Woe.

I am quite worn out."—" Why should I not?" replied the rich man. " We can well afford it, only you must come and work it out with me all this week."— "Willingly," said the poor man; so he set to work, swept out the yard, curried the horses, and split up firewood. At the end of the week the rich brother gave him a *grisenka*[1] in money and a large lump of bread. "Thanks even for that," said the poor man, and was about to turn away homewards, when his brother's conscience evidently pricked him, and he said, "Why dost thou slip off like that? To-morrow is my name day; stay and feast with us." And the poor man stayed to his brother's banquet. But, unfortunately for him, a great many rich guests assembled at his brother's—men of renown; and these guests his brother served most zealously, bowing down low before them, and imploring them as a favour to be so good as to eat and drink their fill. But he forgot altogether about his poor brother, who could only look on from afar, and see all the good people eating and drinking, and enjoying themselves, and making merry. At last the banquet was over, the guests arose, they began to thank the host and hostess, and the poor man also bowed to his very girdle. The guests also went home, and very merry they all were; they laughed, and joked, and sang

[1] Worth about $2\frac{1}{2}d$.

songs all the way. And the poor man went home as hungry as ever, and he thought to himself, "Come, now, I will sing a song too, so that people may think that I too was not overlooked or passed over on my brother's name day, but ate to surfeit, and drank myself drunk with the best of them." And so the peasant began singing a song, but suddenly his voice died away. He heard quite plainly that some one behind his back was imitating his song in a thin piping voice. He stopped short, and the voice stopped short; he went on singing, and again the voice imitated him. "Who is that singing? come forth!" shrieked the poor man, and he saw before him a monster, all shrivelled up and yellow, with scarcely any life in it, huddled up in rags, and girded about with the same vile rags, and its feet wound round with linden bast. The peasant was quite petrified with horror, and he said to the monster, "Who art thou?"—"I am Gore-Gorinskoe; I have compassion on thee; I will help thee to sing."— "Well, Gore, let us go together through the wide [1] world arm in arm; I see that I shall find no other friends and kinsmen there."—"Let us go, then, master; I will never desert thee."—"And on what shall we go, then?"—"I know not what you are going upon, but I will go upon you," and flop! in

---

[1] *Lit.* white world.

an instant he was on the peasant's shoulders. The peasant had not strength enough to shake him off. And so the peasant went on his way, carrying Woeful Woe on his shoulders, though he was scarce able to drag one leg after the other, and the monster was singing all the time, and beating time to it, and driving him along with his little stick. "I say, master, wouldst thou like me to teach thee my favourite song?

> I am Woe, the woefully woeful!
> Girt about with linden bast rags,
> Shod with beggars' buskins, bark stript.
> Live with me, then; live with Woe,
> And sorrow never know.
> If you say you have no money,
> You can always raise it, honey;
> Yet provide a hard-won penny
> 'Gainst the day thou'lt not have any.

And besides," added Woe, "thou already hast this penny against an evil day, besides a crust of bread; let us, then, go on our way, and drink and be merry." So they went on and on, and drank and drank, and so they got home. There sat the wife and all the children, without food, weeping, but Woe set the peasant a-dancing. On the following day Woe began to sigh, and said, "My head aches from drinking!" and again he called upon the master to drink a thimbleful. "I have no money," said the peasant.

—" But didn't I tell thee thou canst always raise it, honey? Pawn thy harrow and plough, sledge and cart, and let us drink; we'll have a rare time of it to-day, at any rate." What could he do? The peasant could not rid himself of Woe, so painfully tight did he sit upon him by this time, so he let himself be dragged about by Woe, and drank and idled away the whole day. And on the next day Woe groaned still more, and even began howling, and said, "Come, let us saunter about; let us drink away everything and pawn it. Sell thyself into slavery, and so get money to drink with." The peasant saw that ruin was approaching him, so he had resort to subtlety, and he said to Woeful Woe, "I have heard our old men say that a treasure was buried about here a long time ago, but it was buried beneath such heavy stones that my single strength would be quite unable to raise it; now, if only we could raise this treasure, darling little Woe, what a fine time of loafing and drinking we should have together!"— "Come, then, and let us raise it; Woe has strength enough for everything." So they went all about the place, and they came to a very large and heavy stone; five peasants together could not have moved it from the spot, but our friend and Woe lifted it up at the first go. And lo! beneath the stone there was indeed a coffer dark and heavy, and at the very bottom of this coffer something was sparkling. And the peasant said to Woe, "You just creep into the coffer and get out the gold, and I'll stand here and hold up the stone." So Woe crept into the coffer with great glee, and cried out, "Hie, master, here are riches incalculable! Twenty jars choke-full of gold, all standing one beside the other!" and he handed up to the peasant one of the jars. The peasant took the jar into his lap, and, as at the same time he let the stone fall back into its old place, he shut up Woeful Woe in the coffer with all the gold. "Perish thou and thy riches with thee!" thought the peasant; "no good luck goes along with thee." And he went home to his own, and with the money he got from the jar he bought wood, repaired his cottage, added live-stock to his possessions, and worked harder than ever, and he began to engage in trade, and it went well with him. In a single year he grew so much richer, that in place of his hut he built him a large wooden house. And then he went to town to invite his brother and his wife to the house-warming. "What are you thinking of?" said his rich brother, with a scornful smile. "A little while ago you were naked, and had nothing to eat, and now you are giving house-warmings, and laying out banquets!"—"Well, at one time, certainly, I had nothing to eat, but now, thank God, I am no worse off than you. Come and see."

The next day the rich brother went out into the country to his poor brother, and there on the pebbly plain he saw wooden buildings, all new and lofty, such as not every town merchant can boast of. And the poor brother who dwelt on the pebbles fed the rich brother till he could eat no more, and made him drink his fill; and after that, when the strings of his tongue were loosened, he made a clean breast of it, and told his brother how he had grown so rich. Envy overcame the rich brother. He thought to himself, "This brother of mine is a fool. Out of twenty kegs he only took one. With all that money Woe itself is not terrible. I'll go there myself, I'll take away the stone, take the money, and let Woe out from beneath the stone. Let him hound my brother to death if he likes." No sooner said than done. The rich man took leave of his brother, but, instead of going home, he went to the stone. He pulled and tugged at it, and managed at last to push it a little to one side, so as to be able to peep into the coffer, but before he could pull his head back again, Woe had already skipped out, and was sitting on his neck. Our rich man felt the grievous burden on his shoulders, looked round, and saw the frightful monster bestriding him. And Woe shrieked in his ear, "A pretty fellow you are! You wanted to starve me to death in there, did you? You shall not shake me off again in a hurry,

I warrant you. I'll never leave you again."—"Oh, senseless Woe!" cried the rich man, "indeed 'twas not I who placed you beneath that stone, and 'tis not me, the rich man, you should cleave to; go hence, and torment my brother." But Woeful Woe would not listen to him. "No," it screeched, "you lie! You deceived me once, but you shan't do it a second time." And so the rich man carried Woe home with him, and all his wealth turned to dust and ashes. But the poor brother now lives in peace and plenty, and sings jesting ditties of Woe the outwitted.

GO I KNOW NOT WHITHER—FETCH I KNOW NOT WHAT.

By the blue sea, in a certain empire, there dwelt once upon a time a king who was a bachelor, and he had a whole company of archers, and the archers used to go a-hunting with him and shoot the birds that flew about, and provided meat for their master's table. In this company served a youthful archer named Fedot, a clever marksman was he, never missing his aim, wherefore the King loved him better than all his comrades. One day he chanced to go a-hunting very early, even at break of day. He went into a dense, drear forest, and there he saw a dove sitting on a tree. Fedot stretched his bow, took aim, fired and broke one of the dove's little wings, and the bird fell from the tree down upon the damp earth. The marksman picked it up, and was about to twist its neck and put it in his pouch, when the dove thus spoke to him: "Alas! young marksman! do not twist my poor little silly neck; drive me not out of the white world. 'Twere better to take me alive, carry me home, put me in thy little window, and lo! the moment that slumber comes over me, at that very moment, I say, stroke me the wrong side down with thy right hand, and great good fortune shall be thine!" The marksman was much amazed. "Why, what is this?" thought he. "Mine eyes tell me 'tis a bird, and naught else, yet it speaks with a human voice! Such a thing has never happened to me before." So he took the bird home, placed it in the window-sill, and waited and waited. 'Twas not very long before the bird laid its head beneath its wing and began to doze. Then the marksman raised his right hand and stroked it, quite lightly, the wrong side down. The dove instantly fell to the ground and became a maiden-soul, and so beautiful that the like of it can only be told in tales, but is neither to be imagined nor guessed at. And she spoke to the good youth who was the royal archer, and said: "Thou hast had wit enough to win me, have also wit enough to live with me. Thou art my predestined husband, I am thy pre-ordained wife." They were immediately of one mind. Fedot married, lived at home, and rejoiced in his young wife, yet forgot not his service either. Every morning, before break of day, he took his weapon, went into the forest, shot various kinds of wild beasts, and took them to the royal kitchen. But it was plain that his wife was much tormented by these hunting expeditions, and one day she said to him: "Listen, my friend! I am fearful for thee! Every blessed day thou dost cast thyself into the forest, dost wander through fen and morass, and returnest home wet through and through, and we are none the better for it. What sort of a trade dost thou call this! Look now, I have a plan whereby thou also shalt profit by it. Get me now a hundred or two of rubles, and I'll manage all the rest." Then Fedot hastened to his comrades, and borrowed a ruble from one, and two rubles from another till he had collected about two hundred rubles. These then he brought to his wife. "Now," said she, "buy me various kinds of silk with all this money!" The archer went and bought various kinds of silk with the two hundred rubles. She took them and said: "Be not sorrowful! Pray God and lay thee down to sleep, the morning is wiser than the evening!" So the husband fell asleep, and the wife went out upon the balcony, opened her book of spells, and immediately two invisible youths appeared before her and said: "What art thou pleased to command?"—"Take this silk, and in a single hour weave me a carpet more wondrous than anything to be found in the wide world, and let the whole kingdom be embroidered on this carpet, with all its cities and villages and rivers and lakes." Then they set to work and wove the carpet, and it was wondrous to behold, wondrous above everything. In the morning the wife handed the carpet to her husband. "There," said she, "take it to the market-place and sell it to the merchants; but look now! haggle not about the price, but take whatever they offer thee for it." Fedot took the carpet, turned it round, hung it over his arm, and went to the market-place. A merchant saw him, ran up to him at once, and said to him: "Hearken to me, honoured sir, wilt thou not sell me that carpet?"—"Willingly!"—"And what then is the price?"—"Thou art a frequenter of the marts, therefore will I leave the price to thee!" The merchant fell a-thinking and a-thinking, he could not price the carpet—he was at his wits' end. Another merchant came running up, and after him a third and a fourth till a great crowd of them collected; they looked at the carpet, marvelled at it, and could not fix the price. At that moment the royal steward passed by that way, saw the crowd, and wanted to know what all the merchants were talking about. So he went up to them and said, "What is the matter?" —"We cannot price this carpet," said they. The steward looked at the carpet, and he also was amazed. "Hearken, archer!" said he, "tell me the real truth; where didst thou get this lordly carpet?"—"My wife wrought it!"—"How much dost thou want for it?"—"I myself know not the value of it; my wife bade me not to haggle over it, but to take whatever was offered."—"Then what dost thou say to 10,000 rubles?" The archer took the money and gave up the carpet. Now this steward was always by the King, and ate and drank at his table. So he went to dine with the King now also, and took the carpet with him. "Would it please your Majesty to look at the carpet I have bought to-day?" The King looked, and saw there his whole realm just as if it were on the palm of his hand, and he heaved a great sigh. "Why, what a carpet is this! In all my life I have never seen such cunning craft. Say now, what wilt thou take for this carpet?" And the King drew out 25,000 rubles and gave them into the hand of the steward, but the carpet they hung up in the palace. "That is a mere nothing," thought the steward, "I'll make a much better thing out of the second chance." So he immediately went in search of the archer, sought out his little hut, entered the dwelling-room, and the moment he saw the archer's wife, at that very instant he forgot all about himself and the errand on which he had come. Nevertheless the steward manned himself with a great effort and turned sullenly homewards. From henceforth he bungled over everything he took in hand, and whether asleep or awake, he thought only of one thing, the wonderfully lovely little archeress.

The King observed the change in him, and asked him, "What ails thee? Has any great grief befallen thee?"—"Alas! my king and father, I have seen the wife of the archer—such a beauty the world knows not of nor has ever seen!" The King himself was seized with a desire to fall in love with her, and he also went to the abode of the archer. He entered the living-room, and sees before him a lady of a loveliness unspeakable. "Love's burning chilblain oppressed his heart." "Why should I remain a bachelor any longer?" thought he; "lo! now, I'll marry this beauty, she's too good for a mere archer. From her birth she was evidently meant to be a Queen!"

The King returned to his palace and said to the steward, "Hearken! thou hast had wit enough to show me the archer's wife, that unspeakable beauty; thou must now have wit enough to remove the husband out of the way. I want to marry her myself. And if thou dost not remove him, look to thyself; although thou art my faithful servant, thou shalt be hanged upon a gallows!" Then the steward went about much more afflicted than before, and think as he would, he could not devise a method of getting rid of the archer. He wandered about the broad marketplaces and the narrow lanes, and there met him one day a miserable old hag. "Stay, thou King's servant!" cried she. "I can see all thy thoughts, thou wantest help against thy unavoidable woe."—"Ah, help me, dear little granny! I'll pay thee what thou wilt!" —"Thou hast received the royal command to get rid of Fedot the archer. The thing is not so very easy. He indeed is simple, but his wife is frightfully artful. Well now, we'll hit upon an errand which will not be accomplished so speedily. Go to the King and say that he must command the archer *to go I know not whither, and fetch I know not what*. Such a task as that he'll never accomplish, though he live for ever and ever; either he will vanish out of knowledge altogether, or if he does come back, it will be without arms or legs." The steward rewarded the old hag with gold, and hastened back to the King, and the King sent and commanded the archer to be brought before him. "Well, Fedot! thou art my young warrior, and the first in my corps of archers. Render me then this service: *Go I know not whither, and fetch me I know not what!* And mark me, if thou bring it me not back, 'tis I, the King, who say it to thee, thy head shall be severed from thy shoulders." The archer turned to the left, quitted the palace, and came home very sad and thoughtful. And his wife asked him: "Why art thou so sorrowful, darling; has any misfortune befallen thee?"—"The King has sent me I know not whither to fetch I know not what. 'Tis through thy beauty that this ruin has come upon us!"—"Yes, indeed! this service is no light one! It takes nine years to get there, and nine years to get back again, eighteen years in all, and God only knows if it can be managed even then!"—"What's to be done then, and what will become of me?"—"Pray God and lie down to sleep, the morning is wiser than the evening. To-morrow thou wilt know all." The archer lay down to sleep, and his wife sat watching till midnight, opened her book of spells, and the two youths immediately appeared before her. "What is thy pleasure, and what thy command?"—"Do ye know how one can manage to go I know not whither, and fetch I know not what?"—"No, we do not know." She closed the book, and the youths disappeared from before her eyes. In the morning the archeress awoke her husband. "Go to the King," said she, "and ask for gold from the treasury for thy journey. Thou hast a pilgrimage of eighteen years before thee. When thou hast the money, come back to me to say farewell." The archer went to the King, received a whole purseful of money, and returned to say good-bye to his wife. She gave him a pocket-handkerchief and a ball, and said: "When thou goest out of the town, throw this ball in front of thee, and whithersoever it rolls, follow it. Here too is my pocket-handkerchief; when thou dost wash thyself, wherever thou mayst be, always dry thy face with this handkerchief." The archer took leave of his wife and of his comrades, bowed low on all four sides of him, and went beyond the barriers of the city. He threw the ball in front of him; the ball rolled and rolled, and he followed hard after it.

A month or so passed away, and then the King called the steward and said to him: "The archer has departed to wander about the wide world for eighteen years, and it is plain that he will not return alive. Now eighteen years are not two weeks, and no little disaster may have befallen him by the way; go then to the archer's house and bring me his wife to the palace!" So the steward went to the archer's house, entered the room, and said to the beautiful archeress: "Hail, thou wise woman! The King commands thee to present thyself at court!" So to the court she went. The King received her with joy and led her into his golden halls, and said to her: "Wilt thou be a Queen? I will make thee my spouse!"—"Where was such a thing ever seen, where was such a thing ever heard of, to take a wife away from her living husband? Though he be nothing but a simple archer, he is for all that my lawful husband."—"If thou come not willingly, I'll take thee by force!" But the beauty laughed, stamped upon the floor, turned into a dove, and flew out of the window.

The archer passed through many countries and kingdoms, and the ball kept rolling ever onwards. Whenever they came to a river the ball expanded into a bridge, and whenever the archer wished to rest, the ball widened into a downy bed. Whether the time be long or whether it be short the tale is quickly told, though the deed be not quickly done; suffice it to say that at last the archer came to a vast and wealthy palace; the ball rolled right up against the door and vanished. The archer fell a-thinking. "I had better go straight on," thought he, so he went up the staircase into a room, and there met him there three lovely damsels. "Whence and wherefore hast thou come hither, good man?" said they. "Alas! lovely damsels, ye ask me not to rest from my long journey, but ye begin to torment me with questionings. First ye should give me to eat and drink and let me rest, and then only should ye ask me of my tidings!" They immediately laid the table, gave him to eat and drink, and made him lie down to rest. The archer slept away his weariness, rose from his soft bed, and the lovely damsels brought him a washing-basin and an embroidered towel. He washed himself in the clear spring-water, but the towel he would not take. "I have my handkerchief wherewith to wipe my face," said he, and he drew out the handkerchief and began to dry himself. And the lovely damsels fell a-questioning him. "Tell us, good man! whence hast thou got that handkerchief?"—"My wife gave it to me."—"Then thou must have married one of our kinswomen." Then they called their old mother, and she looked at the handkerchief, recognizing it the same instant, and cried: "This is indeed my daughter's handkerchief!" Then she began to put all manner of questions to the archer. He told her how he had married her daughter, and how the King had sent him *I know not whither, to fetch I know not what.* "Alas! my dear son-in-law, not even I have heard of this marvel. But come now, perchance my servants may know of it." Then the old woman fetched her book of spells, turned over the leaves, and immediately there appeared two giants. "What is thy pleasure, and what is thy command?"—"Look now, my faithful servants, carry me together with my son-in-law to the wide sea Ocean, and place us in the very centre of it—in the very abyss." Immediately the giants caught up the archer and the old woman, and bore them, as by a hurricane, to the wide sea Ocean, and placed them in the centre of it—in the very abyss; there they stood like two vast columns, and held the archer and the old woman in their arms. Then the old woman cried with a loud voice, and there came swimming up to her all the fish and creeping things of the sea, so that the blue sea was no longer to be seen for the multitude of them. "Hark! ye fishes and creeping things of the sea. Ye who swim everywhere, have ye perchance heard how to go *I know not whither, to fetch I know not what?*" And all the fishes and creeping things exclaimed with one voice, "No, we have never heard of it." Suddenly a lame old croaking frog forced its way to the front and said, "Kwa, kwa; I know where this marvel is to be found."—"Well, dear, that is just what I want to know," said the old woman, and she took up the frog and bade the giants carry her and her son-in-law home. In an instant they found themselves in their own courtyard. Then the old woman began to question the frog. "How and by what road can my son-in-law go?" And the frog answered, "This place is at the end of the world—far, far away. I would gladly lead him thither myself, but I am so frightfully old, I can scarcely move my legs. I could not get there in fifty years." The old woman sent for a big jar, filled it with fresh milk, put the frog inside, and said to her son-in-law, "Hold this jar in thy hand and the frog will show thee the way." The archer took the jar with the frog, took leave of his mother-in-law and his sisters-in-law, and set out on his way. On he went, and the frog showed him the way. Whether it be far or near, long or short, matters not; suffice it that he came to the fiery river; beyond this river was a high mountain, and on this mountain a door was to be seen. "Kwa, kwa," said the frog, "let me out of the jar, we must cross over this river." The archer took it out of the jar and placed it on the ground. "Now, my good youth, sit on me. More firmly. Don't be afraid. Thou wilt not smash me." The youth sat on the frog and pressed it to the very earth. The frog began to swell; it swelled and swelled till it was as large as a haystack. All that the archer now thought of was the risk of falling off. "If I fall off it will be the death of me," thought he. The frog, when it had done swelling, took a leap and leaped with one big bound right across the fiery stream, and again made itself quite little. "Now, good youth, go through that door and I'll wait for thee here; thou wilt come into a cavern, and take care to hide thyself well. In a short time two old men will come; listen to what they are saying, and see what they do, and when they are gone, say and do as they." The archer went into the mountain, opened the door, and in the cavern it was dark enough to put one's eyes out. He fumbled his way along and felt all about him with his arms till he felt an empty chest, into which he got and hid himself. And now, after he had waited some time, two old men entered and said: "Hi!

Shmat-Razum![1] come and feed us." At that very instant—there's no telling how—lightning-flashes lit candelabras, it thundered plates and dishes, and various wines and meats appeared upon the table. The old men ate and drank, and then they commanded—" Shmat-Razum! take it all away." And immediately there was nothing, neither table, nor wine, nor meats, and the candelabras all went out. The archer heard the two old men going out, crept out of the chest, and cried: " Hi! Shmat-Razum!"—"What is your pleasure?"—" Feed me." Again everything appeared. The candelabras were lighted, the table was covered, and all the meats and drinks appeared upon it. The archer sat down at the table and said, "Hi! Shmat-Razum. Come, brother, and sit down with me, let us eat and drink together. I can't stand eating all alone." And an invisible voice answered him: "Alas! good man, whence hath God sent thee? 'Tis thirty years since I have served right trustily the two old men here, and during all that time they have never once asked me to sit down with them." The archer looked about him and was amazed. He saw nobody, yet the meats disappeared from the dishes as if some one was sweeping them away, and the wine bottles lifted themselves up, poured themselves into the glasses,

[1] Rogue-Reason, is perhaps the nearest equivalent.

and in a trice the glasses were empty. Then the archer went on eating and drinking, but he said: "Hearken, Shmat-Razum! Wilt thou be my servant? Thou shalt have a good time of it with me."—"Why should I not? I have long been growing weary here, and thou, I see, art a good man."—"Well, get everything ready and come with me." The archer came out of the cave, looked around him, and there was nothing. "Shmat-Razum, art thou there?"—"I am here. Fear not. I'll never desert thee." "Right," replied the archer, and he sat him on the frog. The frog swelled out and leaped across the fiery stream; he placed it in the jar, and set off on his return journey. He came to his mother-in-law and made his new servant regale the old woman and her daughters right royally. Shmat-Razum feasted them so bountifully that the old woman very nearly danced for joy, and ordered the frog three jars of fresh milk every nine days for its faithful services. The archer then took leave of his mother-in-law and wended his way homewards. He went on and on till he was utterly exhausted, his swift feet trembled beneath him, and his white arms sank down by his side. "Alas!" said he, "Shmat-Razum, dost thou not see how weary I am? My legs fail me."—"Why didst thou not tell it me long ago? I will bring thee to the place alive and well." And immediately the archer was seized by a whirlwind and carried through the air so quickly that his hat fell from his head. "Hi! Shmat-Razum! Stop a minute. My hat has fallen from my head."—"Too late, master. Thou canst not get it. Thy cap is now 5000 miles behind thee." Towns and villages, rivers and forests, melted away beneath the feet of the archer.

And now the archer was flying over the deep sea, and Shmat-Razum said to him: "An thou wilt let me, I would make a golden bower on this sea, and thou wilt be able to rest and be happy!"—"Do so then," said the archer, and straightway they began descending towards the sea. Then, for a moment, the waves splashed high, and then an islet appeared, and on the islet was a golden pleasure-house. Shmat-Razum said to the archer: "Sit in this pleasure-house and rest and look out upon the sea; three merchant vessels will sail by and stop at the islet. Thou must invite the merchants hither, hospitably entertain them, and exchange me for three wondrous things which the merchants will bring with them. In due time I will return to thee again." The merchant kept watch, and lo! from the west three ships came sailing up, and the merchantmen saw the islet and the golden pleasure-house. "'Tis a marvel!" said they; "how many times have we not sailed hither, and nothing was to be seen but the sea! and now, behold! a golden pleasure-house is here. Come, friends, let us put to shore and feast our eyes upon it!" So immediately they lowered the sails and cast the anchor, three of the merchants sat them in a light skiff, and they came to the shore. "Hail, good man!"— "Hail, ye wayfaring merchants, ye men of many marts! be so good as to turn in to me, stroll about at your ease, make merry and repose; this pleasure-house was built expressly for guests that come by sea!" The merchants entered the bower and sat them down on footstools. "Hi! Shmat-Razum!" cried the archer; "give us to eat and drink." The table appeared, and on the table was wine and savoury meats; whatever the soul desired was there with the wishing. The merchants sighed for envy. "Come," said they, "let us make an exchange. Thou give us thy servant, and take from us what marvels thou likest best."—"But what marvels have ye then?"—"Look and see!" And one of the merchants drew out of his pocket a little casket, and he had no sooner opened it than a lovely garden spread out all over the island with fragrant flowers and pleasant paths; but when he shut the casket the garden immediately disappeared. The second merchant drew from beneath the folds of his garment an axe, and began to tap with it: "Rap-tap!" out came a ship. "Rap-tap!" out came another ship. A hundred times he rapped, and made a hundred ships with sails and guns and crews complete; the ships sailed, the sailors stood by the guns and took orders from the merchant. The merchant gloried in it for a while, but then he concealed his axe and the ships vanished out of sight just as if they had never been. The third merchant produced a horn, blew into one end of it, and immediately an army appeared, both horse and foot, with cannons and banners, and through all the ranks went the roll of martial music, and the armour of the warriors flashed like fire in the sunlight. The merchant rejoiced in it all, then he took his horn and blew into the other end of it, and there was nothing to be seen, the whole of that martial might was no more.

"Your marvels are well enough, but they are of no use to me," said the archer; "your hosts and your fleets would do honour to a Tsar, but I am only a simple archer. If you would change with me, then must you give me all your three wonders in exchange for my one invisible servant."—"But won't that be too much?"—"Know ye that I'll make no other exchange." The merchants considered amongst themselves: "What's the use of this garden, these ships, and these hosts to us? 'Twill be better to make the exchange; at any rate we shall always be able to eat and drink our fill without the least trouble." So they gave the archer their wonders, and said: "Well, Shmat-Razum, we'll take thee with us; wilt thou serve us well and loyally?"—"Why should I not serve you? 'Tis all one with me with whom I live." The merchants returned to their ships and regaled all their crews right royally. "Hi! Shmat-Razum! bestir thyself!" And every one on board ate and drank his fill and lay down and slept heavily. But the archer sat in his golden bower and grew pensive, and said: "Alas! my heart yearns after my faithful servant, Shmat-Razum. I wonder where he is now!" —"I am here, master!" The archer was glad. "Is it not time for us to hasten home?" And he had no sooner spoken than a whirlwind as it were seized him and bore him into the air.

The merchants awoke from their sleep and wanted to drink away the effects of their carouse: "Hi! Shmat-Razum, give us some more drink by way of a pick-me-up!" But no one answered, no one rendered them that service. Order and shout as they might, things remained precisely as they were. "Well, gentlemen! this sharper has befooled us! The devil take him, and may the island vanish and the golden bower perish." Thus the merchants lamented and lamented, then they spread their sails and departed whither their business called them.

The archer flew back to his country, and descended

in a waste place by the blue sea. "Hi, Shmat-Razum, can we not build us a little castle here?"—"Why not? It shall be ready immediately." And immediately the castle sprang up, more beautiful than words can tell, 'twas twice as good as a royal palace. The archer opened his casket and a garden immediately appeared round the castle with pleasant country paths and marvellous flowers. There sat the archer at the open window, and quite fell in love with his garden. Suddenly a dove flew in at the window, plumped down upon the ground, and turned into his lovely young wife. They embraced and greeted each other. And the wife said to the archer, "Ever since thou didst leave the house I have been flying as a blue dove among the woods and groves. How happily we will now live together for evermore!"

Early the next morning the King came out on his balcony and looked towards the blue sea, and behold! on the very shore stood a new castle, and round the castle was a green garden. "Who then is this presumptuous stranger who builds on my land without my leave?" Then his couriers ran thither, asked questions, and came back and told him that this castle was built by the archer, and he himself dwelt in this castle and his wife with him. The King was more angry than ever, and he bade them assemble a host and go to the shores of the sea, root up the garden, smash the castle into little bits, and bring the archer and his wife to him. The archer saw the King's army coming against him, and it was very strong; then he seized his axe quickly and rapped with it, "Rap-tap!" Out came a ship. He rapped one hundred times, and made one hundred ships. Then he seized his horn and blew once, and a host of footmen rolled out. He blew in the other end, and a host of horse rolled out. The commanders of all the corps came rushing up to him, and asked him for orders. The archer bade them begin the battle. The music struck up, the drums rolled, the regiments moved forwards against the royal host. The infantry, like a solid wall, broke down their centre, the horse cut them off at the wings and took them captive, and the guns from the fleet played upon the capital. The King saw that all his host was flying, rushed forward to stop them—but how? He could not do it, and in a moment he was swept from his horse in the midst of the fierce fight and trampled underfoot. When the fight was over the people assembled together and begged the archer to accept the whole realm from their hands. To this he gave his consent, and ruled that kingdom peaceably all the days of his life.

KUZ'MA SKOROBOGATY.[1]

THERE was once a peasant and his wife, and they had one son, and he, though good, was a blockhead, and no good at all for working in the fields. "Husband mine," said the mother, "there is not much wit in our son, and he will eat us out of house and home; send him away, let him live by himself, and make his own way in the world." So they sent away their son; they gave him a most wretched little nag, a tumble-down hut in the wood, and a cock with five hens. And little Kuz'ma lived alone, all alone in the dark wood.

The little she-fox scented out the fowls that were right under her very nose in the wood, and determined to pay a visit to Kuz'ma's hut. One day little Kuz'ma went out to hunt, and no sooner had he left the hut than the little fox, who was on the watch all the time, ran up, killed one of the hens, roasted it, and ate it

[1] Quick-rich.

up. Little Kuz'ma returned, and behold! one of the hens was gone. And he thought: "I suppose the vulture must have pounced down on it!" The next day he again went out hunting. He happened to fall in with the fox, and she asked him: "Whither away, little Kuz'ma?"—"I am going a-hunting, little fox!"—"Well, good-bye!" And immediately she scampered off to his hut, killed another hen, cooked it, and ate it. Little Kuz'ma came home and counted his hens, and another was missing. And it occurred to him: "What if the little fox has tasted of my hens!" On the third day he nailed up the door and window of his hut strongly, so strongly, and went about his business as usual. And the fox turned up from somewhither and said to him: "Whither away, little Kuz'ma?"—"I go a-hunting, little fox!"— "Well, good-bye!" Off she ran to Kuz'ma's hut, and he followed her track back too. The fox ran all round the hut, and saw that the door and window were nailed up strongly, oh so strongly; how was she to get into the hut? So up she climbed and disappeared down the chimney; then up came Kuz'ma and caught the fox. "Ah-ha!" cried he; "look what a thief pays me visits! Wait a bit, my little lady; you shall not get out of my hands alive." Then the little fox began to implore Kuz'ma: "Don't kill me! I'll get thee betrothed to a rich bride. Only please roast me one more fowl, the fattest, with lots of nice oil!" Little Kuz'ma fell a-thinking, and then he killed one more fowl for the little fox: "There, eat, little fox, and much good may it do thee!" The fox ate it up, licked her chaps, and said: "Behind this wood is the tsardom of the great and terrible Tsar Ogon,[1] his wife is the Tsaritsa Molnya,[2] and they have a daughter, a most beauteous Tsarevna; I'll marry thee to her."—"Who would take a poor fellow like me?"—"Silence! that's not thy business." And the little fox set off to Tsar Ogon and the Tsaritsa Molnya. She ran all the way to them, entered their palace, made a low obeisance, and said: "Hail, mighty, potent Tsar Ogon, and terrible Tsaritsa Molnya!"— "Hail to thee, fox! What nice little piece of good news hast thou brought us?"—"Well, I have come to you as a match-maker. You have the bride and I have the young bridegroom, Kuz'ma Skorobogaty."— "Where is he buried that he does not come himself?" —"He cannot quit his principality. He rules over the wild beasts, and takes his pleasure with them." —"So that's the sort of bridegroom you present us with! Well, go back to him and say that he must send us forty forties of gray wolves, and then we'll accept him as the bridegroom." Then the little fox ran to the meadows which lay beneath this very wood

[1] Fire.   [2] Lightning.

and began rolling about in these meadows. A wolf came running up and said: "I see, gossip, that you've had a good feed somewhere or you would not roll about like that."—"I wish I wasn't so full; I've been at a banquet with the Tsar and the Tsaritsa. Do you mean to say that you've not been invited there, gossip? Impossible! Why, all the wild beasts were there, and as for the sables and ermines there was no end to them! The bears were still sitting there when I left, and eating like anything!" The wolf began to beg the fox humbly: "Little fox, can't you take me to the Tsar's banquet!"—"Why not! Hearken! Go you and collect by to-morrow forty forties of your brethren, the gray wolves, and I'll lead the whole lot of you thither." On the following day the wolves assembled and the fox led them to the Tsar's white stone palace, placed them all in rows, and announced to the Tsar: "Mighty and potent Tsar Ogon and terrible Tsaritsa Molnya, thy destined son-in-law has sent thee gifts; lo! a whole herd of gray wolves does obeisance to you, and the number of them is forty forties." The Tsar bade them drive all the wolves into the enclosure, and said to the fox: "If my destined son-in-law is able to send me wolves as a present, let him now also send me just as many bears." The little fox ran to little Kuz'ma and bade him roast another fowl, ate her fill of it, and ran off again to the fenced meadows of the Tsar. Thither she went and fell a-rolling about under the selfsame wood. And out of the wood came running a shaggy bear and looked at the fox. "Well, gossip fox," said he, "you have plainly had your fill, or what has come over you to make you roll about in the grass so merrily?"—"Had my fill! I should think so. Why I've been to the Tsar's banquet; there was a whole lot of us beasts there, and of sables and ermines no end. The wolves are eating there now, and a nice dinner they are making of it." Bruin straightway began to beg the fox to let him go: "Little fox, won't you lead me also to the Tsar's banquet?"— "Very well; hearken. Bring together by to-morrow forty forties of black bears, and I'll lead you thither with pleasure, for of course the Tsar's cooks would not make ready for you alone." Old bandy-legs wandered all about the woods, proclaimed the news to all the bears, and got together as many bears as the fox had commanded, and she led them to the Tsar's white stone palace, arranged them in rows, and announced: "Mighty and potent Tsar Ogon, and terrible Tsaritsa Molnya, your destined son-in-law salutes you with a present of forty forties of black bears." The Tsar bade them drive the bears also into the enclosure, and said to the fox: "If my destined son-in-law can send me so many bears and wolves as a gift, let him now send us also just as many martens and sables." The fox again hastened off to Kuz'ma, bade him roast the last hen, together with the cock, and when she had eaten them in his honour she went again to the fenced meadows of the Tsar, and began rolling about in the grass. A sable and a marten came running by. "Where have you been feeding so fatly, sly Mrs. Foxy?" they asked. "What! ye live in the wood and yet don't know that I am held in great honour by the Tsar? This day I have conducted the wolves and the bears to his banquet; by this time they will be unable to tear themselves away from the Tsar's tit-bits; never have they had such a feed from the day of their birth." Then the sable and the marten also began wheedling the fox. "Dear little dovey gossip! wilt not thou lead us to the Tsar? We will only look on afar off while the others eat."—"If ye will bring together forty forties of your sables and martens a dinner shall be got ready for the whole lot of you. But a couple of you all alone would not even be admitted into the courtyard." The next day the sables and the martens came together, and the fox led them to Tsar Ogon, made obeisance to him on behalf of his future son-in-law, and presented him with the forty forties of sables and martens. The Tsar accepted the gift, and said: "Thanks! Tell my destined son-in-law to come to me himself; we want to have a look at him, and it is time he saw his bride."

The next day the little fox again came running to court. The Tsar asked her: "Where, then, is our destined son-in-law?" The little fox replied: "He bade me bow low before you and say that to-day he cannot manage to come anyhow!"—"How so?" "Well, he is frightfully busy; he is getting together all his things to come to you, and just now he is counting up his treasures. So now he begs you to lend him a corn-measure, he must measure his silver money; his corn-measures are all choke-full of gold." The Tsar, without more ado, gave the fox the corn-measure, but he said to himself: "Well done, fox! This is something like a son-in-law that has fallen to our lot. He actually measures his gold and silver with corn-measures!" The next day the fox again came running to court and returned the Tsar his corn-measure (but she had stuck little silver pieces all about the corners of it), and said: "Your destined son-in-law, Kuz'ma Skorobogaty, bade me bow low to you and say that to-day he'll be with you with all his riches." The Tsar was delighted, and bade them have everything ready for the reception of the precious guest. But the little fox set off for Kuz'ma's hut, and there, for the last two days, Kuz'ma had been lying on the stove—hungry, oh! so hungry, and waiting. The fox said to him: "Why dost thou lie down like that? I have got thee a bride from Tsar Ogon and the Tsaritsa Molnya. Let us come to them as guests and celebrate the wedding!"—"Why, fox! art thou out of thy wits? How can I go when I haven't even clothes to cover me?"—"Go! saddle thy nag, I say! and don't bother thy head about that!" Kuz'ma brought out his sorry jade from beneath the shed, covered it with a mat, put on the reins, jumped on its back, and set off after the fox at a light trot. They were already drawing near to the palace, when they came across a little bridge directly in their path. "Jump off thy horse!" said the fox to Kuz'ma, "and saw through the buttresses of this bridge." So little Kuz'ma fell a-sawing with all his might, and sawed through the buttresses of the bridge. Down came the bridge with a crash. "Now, strip thyself naked, throw thy horse and all thy clothes into the water, and roll about in the sand, and wait for me!" That's what the fox said; and then off she ran to the Tsar and the Tsaritsa, and cried to them from afar: "Hi, dear little father! Such an accident! Help, help!" —"What's the matter, dear little foxy?" asked the Tsar.—"Why, this;. the bridges in your tsardom are not strong enough. Your destined son-in-law was coming to you with all his riches, and this precious bridge broke down beneath the weight of them, and all his wealth and all his people have fallen in, and he himself is lying on the bridge more dead than alive!" The Tsar made a great to-do, and shrieked at his servants, and cried: "Haste ye, haste ye! as quickly as ye can, and take of my royal robes for Kuz'ma Skorobogaty, and save him from mortal harm!" And the envoys of the Tsar ran as fast as they could to the bridge, and there they saw little Kuz'ma rolling about in the sand. They picked him up, washed and dried him all over, arrayed him in the royal robes, curled his hair, and led him respectfully to the palace. The Tsar, full of joy that his destined son-in-law had been delivered from such peril, bade them ring all the bells, fire all the guns, and celebrate the wedding at once. So they crowned Kuz'ma as the groom of the Tsarevna, and he dwelt with his father-in-law, and sang songs all day; and the fox was held in high honour at court till life at court ceased to bore her, and she had no longer any desire to return to the woods.

THE TSAREVNA LOVELINESS-INEXHAUSTIBLE.

A LONG time ago, far from our days, in a certain tsardom in a certain Empire lived a famous Tsar Afron Afronovich, and he had three youthful sons: the eldest the Tsarevich Dimitry, the second the Tsarevich Vasily, and the youngest the Tsarevich Ivan. The sons of Afron were all grown up; the youngest had reached his seventeenth year, while Tsar Afron himself had left sixty years behind him. And once, as Tsar Afron fell a-thinking and looked at his sons, his heart grew sad: "Look now!" thought he, "life is a good thing to these youths, and they rejoice in God's fair world; but, as for me, I feel old age drawing nigh, and divers diseases begin to afflict me, and the wide world has now but little delight for me. How will it be with me henceforth? How shall I escape old age?" Thus he thought and thought, and so he fell asleep. And a vision appeared to the Tsar. Somewhere or other beyond lands thrice-nine, in the Empire of Thrice-ten, dwelt the Tsarevna Loveliness-Inexhaustible, the daughter of three mothers, the granddaughter of three grandmothers, the sister of nine brothers; and under the pillow of this Tsarevna was preserved a flask of living-water, and whoever drank of this water instantly became thirty years younger. No sooner did the Tsar Afron awake from his sleep, than he called together his children and the wise men of his realm, and said to them: "Interpret me this dream, ye my sages and cunning counsellors. What shall I do, and how can I discover this Tsarevna?" The sages were silent. The cunning counsellors stroked their long gray beards, looked up and down, scratched their heads, and thus they answered the Tsar Afron: "Oh, Sovereign Tsar! though we have not seen this thing with our eyes, yet our ears have heard of this Tsarevna Loveliness-Inexhaustible; but how to find her, and which way to get at her, that we know not." No sooner did the three Tsarevichs hear this, when with one voice they thus implored their father the Tsar: "Dear father Tsar! give us thy blessing, and send us to the four corners of the earth, that we may see people and show ourselves and discover the Tsarevna Loveliness-Inexhaustible." The father agreed, gave them provision for the journey, took leave of them tenderly, and sent them off to the four corners of the earth. When the two elder brothers got beyond the city gates they turned to the right, but the youngest brother, the Tsarevich Ivan, turned to the left. The elder brothers had got only a hundred miles and no more from home, when they met an old man, and he asked them: "Whither are ye going, young men? Is your journey far?"—But the Tsareviches replied: "Take yourself off, old rogue! What business is it of yours?" The old man said nothing but went on his way. The Tsarevichs went on and on, all that day and the next and a whole week, and they came to such a wilderness that they could see neither earth nor sky, nor any living being, nor any habitation; and in the deepest depth of this wilderness they met another old man, even older than the first. "Hail, good youths!" said he to the Tsareviches. "Are ye truants and rest, or are ye in quest?"—"Why, we are in quest of something, of course. We are going in search of the Tsarevna Loveliness-Inexhaustible, with her flask of living-water!"—"Nay, my good youths!" said the aged stranger, "'twere better ye did not try to get thither."—"And why, pray?"—"I'll tell you. Three rivers cross this road—rivers large and broad. On these rivers are three ferries. At the first ferry they'll cut off your right arm, at the second your left, but at the third they'll cut off your head!"

The brother Tsareviches were sore distressed, their giddy pates hung down below their sturdy shoulders, and they thought to themselves: "Ought we not to have some regard for our father's head and our own heads also? 'Twill be much better to return home alive and well, and wait for fine weather by the sea." And they turned back; and when they were a twenty-four hours' journey from home, they resolved to rest in the fields; and they spread their tents, with the golden tent-poles, let their horses out to graze, and said: "Here we'll stop and await our brother, and while away the time in idleness."

But with the Tsarevich Ivan it fared far otherwise on his journey. There met him the same old man who had encountered his brothers, and this old man asked him the self-same question: "Whither art thou going, young man? Is thy journey far?" And the Tsarevich Ivan answered him: "What is that to thee? I want to have nothing to say to thee!"—But afterwards, when he had gone on a little further, he bethought him of what he had done. "Why did I answer the old man so rudely? Old people are full of ideas! perchance he might have advised me well." So he turned his horse, overtook the old man, and said: "Stay, my father! I did not quite hear what thou saidst to me."—"I asked thee whether thy journey was far?"—"Well, my father, the fact is, I am in search of the Tsarevna Loveliness-Inexhaustible, the daughter of three mothers, the granddaughter of three grandmothers, the sister of nine brothers. I want to get from her the living-water for my dad the Tsar."—"Well," said the old man, "'tis well for thee, good youth, that thou hast answered courteously, and therefore I will put thee in the right way. But thou wilt never get there on an ordinary horse."—"Then whence shall I get me an extraordinary horse?"—"I'll tell thee. Return home, and bid your grooms drive all thy father's horses down to the blue sea, and whichever horse breaks away from the others and goes right into the sea up to his neck, and begins to drink till the blue sea begins to rise and dash from shore to shore—him seize and mount." "I thank thee for thy good words, my father." The Tsarevich did as the old man bade him. He chose the most valiant charger from among his father's horses, watched all through the night, and when on the following morning he went out and mounted into the saddle, the horse spoke to him, with a man's voice: "Tsarevich Ivan, dismount! I will buffet thee thrice, to give thee the muscles of a hero." He buffeted once, he buffeted twice, but the third time he buffeted not at all. "I see," cried he, "that if I were to buffet thee a third time, the whole land would not be able to hold us both." Then the Tsarevich Ivan sat on the horse, put on knightly armour, took out of the armoury of his father's palace an old heroic, trusty blade, and set out upon his quest. He went for a day and for a night, for a month, and for two months, and three; and so he came to a place where his horse was in water up to the knees, and in grass up to the breast, while he, poor youth, had nothing to eat. And in the midst of this wilderness the Tsarevich Ivan found a miserable hut; this hut stood upon fowl's legs, and in it was the Baba-Yaga; the bony-legged witch was lying down, and her legs stretched from corner to corner. The Tsarevich went into the hut and cried: "Hail, Granny!"—"Hail to thee, Tsarevich Ivan; hast come to rest, or art thou in quest?"—"I am in quest of something, Granny. I am off beyond lands thrice-nine, to the Empire of Thrice-ten, I seek the Tsarevna Loveliness-Inexhaustible. I want to get from her the living-water for my dad, the Tsar." The Baba-Yaga answered: "Though I have not seen it with my eyes, I have heard of it with my ears; but thou wilt never get there."—"Wherefore?"—"Because there, there are three ferries; at the first they'll cut off thy right hand, at the second thy left, and at the third thy head."—"Well, Granny, one single head is not such a great matter. I'll go—and God's will be done!"—"Alas, O Tsarevich Ivan! 'twere much better to turn back; thou art still young and tender, thou hast never been in dangerous places, thou hast never run great terrors."—"Nay, Granny! He who tugs at the rope must not cry, I'm broke!"[1] So he took leave of the Baba-Yaga and went on further, and he came at last to the first ferry, and he saw the ferrymen on the other side, lying down asleep. The Tsarevich Ivan stood on the bank and thought to himself: "If I call to them, I shall deafen them for ever, and if I whistle with all my might, I shall upset the ferry-boat." So he whistled a half whistle, and immediately the ferrymen started from their slumber and rowed him across the stream. "What do ye want for your labours, my friends?" asked the Tsarevich Ivan.—"Well, what's the use of haggling? Give us your right arm!" cried the ferrymen, with one voice.—"Nay, nay; I want my arm for myself!" cried the Tsarevich Ivan; and drawing forth his stout blade, he struck to the right and to the left, and beat all the ferrymen till they were half dead, and then went on further. And in this way he crossed the other two fords also. At last he came to the Empire of Thrice-ten, and on the borders of it stood a wild man, in stature like a tree of the forest, as thick-set as a haystack; there he stood, and in his hand he held a club of oak. And the Giant said to

---

[1] He who has said A, must say B also.

the Tsarevich Ivan: "Whither art thou going, oh worm?"—"I am going to the realm of the Tsarevna Loveliness-Inexhaustible, to get the living-water for my father, the Tsar."—"What, thou pigmy! I've been guarding her realm here these hundred years. I have had my fill of heroes—not like thee were the youths who came hither, yet they all fell beneath my hand, and their bones all lie over there. But as for thee, thou art a mere worm!" The Tsarevich saw that he could not overcome the giant, so he turned his horse aside. He went on and on till he came to the very depths of the forest, till he came upon a hut, and in this hut sat a very old, old woman. The moment she saw the good youth she cried: "Hail! Tsarevich Ivan, why hath God sent thee hither?" The Tsarevich told her all his secrets. The old woman had pity on him, and drew from her stove a magic poisonous weed and a little ball. "Go into the open plain," said she, "rake up a fire, and throw this magic poisonous weed into it. But mark me now; stand thou at the back of the blast, lest the smoke from the fire blow upon thee. This blast will cause the giant to be overcome by a deep sleep; then do thou cut off his head, but roll the ball before thee and follow whithersoever it rolls. The ball will lead thee to those very places where reigns the Tsarevna Loveliness-Inexhaustible. The Tsarevna walks about there for nine days, and on the tenth day after that she will refresh herself with the sleep of heroes in her own place. But look to it that thou dost not enter in by the gate, but leap right over the wall with all thy might, and do not stick in the strings at the top of the wall, lest thou arouse the whole empire, when thou wilt not escape alive. But the moment thou hast leaped over the wall, go straight into the palace —into the back-chamber; open the door very, very softly, and draw out the flask of living-water from beneath the pillow of the Tsarevna. But when thou hast got the flask, hasten back as quickly as thou camest, nor look for an instant upon the beauty of the Tsarevna, lest it be too much for thee, good youth!" The Tsarevich Ivan thanked the old woman, and did everything she bade him. As soon as he had lit the fire, he threw the weed into it so that the smoke spread in the direction where the wild man was standing on guard; the eyes of the giant grew dim, he began to yawn and stretch, he laid him on the damp earth and began to sleep soundly—very soundly. The Tsarevich Ivan cut off his head, rolled the little ball along, and went on further. He went on and on, and far away the golden palace began to gleam amidst the green of the forest. All at once a column of dust came out of the palace and along the road, and the gleam of lances and

Tsarevna Loveliness Inexhaustible.

cuirasses was visible through the dust, and there was a sound as of the trampling of many warlike chargers. The little ball rolled out of the road a little on one side; the Tsarevich Ivan, following after it, also turned from the path, went among the bushes, and let his horse out to grass. And from his place in the bushes he saw approaching the Tsarevna Loveliness-Inexhaustible, and she diverted herself with her warriors in the green meadows. And the whole of the Tsarevna's array consisted of maidens alone, each one more beautiful than her neighbour. But the most lovely of them all was the inexhaustibly lovely Tsarevna. She pitched her tent in the meadows, and for nine days she and her maidens diverted themselves with divers pastimes. But the Tsarevich, like a hungry wolf, looked out from his hiding-place at the Tsarevna, he could not take his eyes from her, and look as he might he could not look his fill. At last, on the tenth day, when every one in the Tsarevna's golden courts was asleep, he, spurring his horse with all his might, leaped right over the wall into the garden-court of the ladies, fastened his horse to a wooden post, and stealthily as a thief made his way into the palace, right into the very cabinet where, extended on her downy bed, with her fair locks scattered all about, lay the Tsarevna Loveliness-Inexhaustible, sleeping an unwakable heroic sleep. The Tsarevich drew from under her pillow the flask with the living-water, and was about to run off as quickly as he could, but it was too much for his youthful heart, and leaning over the Tsarevna, he kissed her thrice on her lips, which were sweeter than sugar. And by the time he had got out of the chamber, mounted his horse, and leaped across the wall, she awoke from his kisses. Loveliness-Inexhaustible leaped on her swift-flying mare, and hastened after the Tsarevich Ivan. The Tsarevich urged on his good steed, pulled at the silken reins, and lashed its sides with his whip. And the horse spoke to him with a man's voice: "Wherefore dost thou beat me, Tsarevich Ivan? Neither the fowls of the air nor the beasts of the forest can escape or hide from that mare. She runs so that the earth trembles, she leaps across swift rivers from shore to shore, hills and dales vanish away beneath her feet!" And it had only time to speak these words when the Tsarevna overtook the good youth, struck him with her swinging blade, and pierced him full in the breast. Down fell the Tsarevich Ivan from his horse on the moist ground; his bright eyes closed, his red blood flowed. Loveliness-Inexhaustible gazed into his eyes, and a great sorrow overcame her; she saw that such a lovely youth as that was not to be found in the wide world. And she placed her white hand on the wound, washed it with living-water out of her flask, and immediately the wound healed up, and the Tsarevich Ivan arose well and unharmed.—" Wilt thou take me to wife?"—"That I will, Tsarevna!" —" Then return to thy kingdom, and if after three years thou hast not forgotten me, I will be thy wife, and thou shalt be my husband." And the destined bridegroom took leave of his bride, and they parted in different directions. The Tsarevich Ivan went on and on for a long time, and saw many things, and at last he came upon a tent on a mountain, with a golden tent-pole, and round the tent two good horses were feeding on white summer-wheat and drinking mead, and in the tent were lying his two elder brothers, eating and drinking and diverting themselves with manifold diversions. And the elder brothers began to ask the younger one : " Hast thou got the living-water for our father?"—" I have got it!" replied the Tsarevich Ivan simply, for he always spoke out his secrets, happen what might. The elder brothers invited him to feast with them, made him drunk, drew the flask of living-water out of his bosom, and threw him down a precipice. The Tsarevich Ivan flew down and down, and at last he fell into the Realm-beneath-the-Earth. "And now," thought he, "irretrievable ruin has come upon me! I can never find the ways that lead from hence!" So he went about in the Realm-beneath-the-Earth. He went on and on, and saw that the day grew shorter and shorter till it was like night; and at last he came to a place that was not a desert, and by the sea stood a castle that was a town, and a hut that was a mansion. The Tsarevich went up a flight of steps into a barn, and from the barn he went into the hut, prayed to God, and begged for a good night's rest. But in the hut sat an old woman—an old, a very old woman; she was all wrinkled and gray. "Good youth," cried she, "thou mayest sleep there and welcome; but say! how didst thou get hither?"—"Thou art an old person, granny, but thy way of asking is not wise. Thou shouldst first give me to eat and drink, and let me lie down to sleep, and after that ask me concerning my tidings." The old woman gave the Tsarevich to eat and drink, let him lie down to sleep, and then asked him again. And the Tsarevich Ivan said to her: "I have been in the Kingdom of Thrice-ten, as the guest of the Tsarevna Loveliness-Inexhaustible, and now I am returning home to my father the Tsar Afron, but I have wandered from my path. Canst thou not show me the way home?"—"I do not know it myself, Tsarevich. Here have I been living nine-tenths of my life on this earth, and I have never heard of the Tsar Afron. Come now! sleep in peace, and to-morrow I will bring together my messengers, perhaps one of them may know." The next day the

Tsarevich got up very early, washed himself quite white, and went out with the old woman on the balcony, and the old woman cried with a piercing voice: "Hi, hi! ye swimming fish of the sea, and ye creeping reptiles of the earth, my faithful servants, assemble here to the very last one of you!" And immediately the blue sea was disturbed and all the fishes assembled, both small and great, and all the reptiles assembled; they all came to the shore under the water. "Does any one know where in all the world dwells the Tsar Afron, and by what way one can get to his kingdom from here?" And all the fishes and reptiles answered with one voice: "We have neither seen it with our eyes, nor heard it with our ears." Then the old woman turned to the other side and screeched: "Hi! ye wandering beasts of the forest, and ye fowls that fly in the air, my trusty servants, assemble hither, and fly and run hither all of you, down to the very last one!" And the beasts of the forest came running in bands and bands, and the fowls of the air came flying in flocks and flocks, and the old woman began to ask them about Tsar Afron; and they all with one voice exclaimed to the old woman: "We have neither seen it with our eyes, nor heard it with our ears."—"Well, Tsarevich, there's nobody else to ask now, we've asked them all." They were just about to go into the hut again, when there was a whistling and a roaring sound in the air, and the bird Mogol came flying along; he hid the light of day with his wings, and lighted on the ground close to the hut. "Where hast *thou* been, and why art thou come so late?" screeched the old woman. "I have been flying a long way off, in the realm of Tsar Afron, at the uttermost end of the wide world."—"Well, thou art just the one I want; render me now true and loyal service: carry thither the Tsarevich Ivan."—"I shall be glad to carry him, but I shall want heaps and heaps of food; it takes three years to fly thither."—"Take as much as thou dost want." And the old woman made provision for the journey of the Tsarevich Ivan. She placed upon the bird a hogshead of water, and on the top of it a wicker basket full of meat, and put into his hands an iron pole. "There," said she, "when thou fliest on the bird Mogol and she turns round and looks at thee, immediately plunge thy pole into the basket and give her a piece of beef." The Tsarevich Ivan said "thank you" to the old woman, sat on the bird, and immediately she rose with him and bore him up in the air like a whirlwind. She flew and flew, she flew for a long, long time, and whenever she looked round at the Tsarevich he fed her with beef off the pole. And at last the Tsarevich Ivan saw that the basket was getting empty, so he said to the bird Mogol:

"Look now, thou bird Mogol! thou hast now but little food left; light upon the moist earth, and I'll get thee another basketful of divers meats." But the bird Mogol answered and said: "Art thou mad, Tsarevich Ivan? Beneath us now is a forest dark and drear, muddy and boggy; if we lighted down there, thou and I would never get out again so long as the world lasts." And now the Tsarevich had dispensed all the meat from the basket, and sent the basket and the hogshead flying off the bird; but the bird Mogol still kept on flying and turning its head for food. What was to be done now? The Tsarevich Ivan cut off the calves of his legs, put them on the pole, and gave them to the bird Mogol. She swallowed them up, and descended with the Tsarevich Ivan into a green meadow, upon silky grass with azure flowers. As the Tsarevich Ivan leaped off her on to the ground, the bird Mogol coughed up his calves again, fastened them on to his legs, moistened them with her spittle, and the Tsarevich went on his way well and strong. He came to the capital of Tsar Afron, his own father, and saw that something amiss was going on in the town. Crowds of people were wandering about the streets from end to end, the Tsar's cunning counsellors were strolling aimlessly about the city, asking something from every one they met, and shaking their gray heads as if they were out of their wits. And the Tsarevich asked one of the people he met: "What's the meaning of all this commotion in the city?" And the good people answered him: "The Tsarevna Loveliness-Inexhaustible is sailing against our kingdom; she is bringing a countless host with her in forty ships, and she demands that the Tsar should surrender to her the Tsarevich Ivan who disturbed her sleep three years ago by kissing her on her lips, which are sweeter than sugar; and if we do not surrender him she will destroy our kingdom utterly with fire and sword."—"Well, it seems to me I have come just in time. I want this Tsarevna just as much as she wants me." And he immediately went on board the Tsarevna's ship. Here they embraced and fondled each other, and received their bridal crowns in the church of God, and after that they went to the Tsar Afron and told him all. The Tsar Afron drove his elder sons from Court, deprived them of their inheritance, and lived with his younger son, and lived happily and increased in all riches.

VERLIOKA.

THERE was once upon a time an old man and an old woman, and they had two orphan grandchildren so lovely, gentle, and good, that the old man and the old woman could not love them enough. The old man once took it into his head to go out into the fields with his grandchildren to look at the peas, and they saw that their peas were growing splendidly. The old man rejoiced at the sight with his grandchildren, and said: "Well, now, you won't find peas like that in the whole world! By and by we'll make kisel[1] out of it, and bake us some pea-cakes." And next morning the grandfather sent the eldest grandchild, and said: "Go and drive away the sparrows from the peas!" The grandchild sat down beside the peas, shook a dry branch, and kept on saying, "Whish! whish! sparrows, ye have pecked at grandfather's peas till you're quite full!" And all at once

[1] A sourish meat-pottage.

she heard a rumbling and a roaring in the wood, and Verlioka came, huge of stature, with one eye, a hooked nose, ragged stubbly hair, moustaches half an ell long, swine's bristles on his head, hobbling on one leg, in a wooden boot, leaning on a crutch, grinding all his teeth, and smiling. He went up to the pretty little grandchild, seized her and dragged her away with him behind the lake. The grandfather waited and waited, but there was no grandchild, and he sent his young grandson after her. Verlioka walked off with him also. The grandfather waited and waited, and said to his wife: "How very late our grandchildren are! I suppose they are running about there and idling their time away, or catching starlings with some lads or other, and meanwhile the sparrows are looting our peas! Go along, old woman, and teach them sense!" The old woman rose from the stove, took her stick from the corner, gave the pasties another turn, went away—and never came back. As soon as Verlioka saw her in the field, he cried: "What dost thou want here, old hag? Hast thou come hither to shell peas? Then I'll make thee stand here among the peas for ever and ever!" Then he set to work belabouring her with his crutch, till little by little her very soul oozed out of her, and she lay upon the field more dead than alive.

The grandfather waited in vain for his grandchildren and his old wife, and began to scold at them: "Where on earth have they got to!" said he; "'tis a true saying that a man must expect no good from his ribs." Then the old man himself made his way to the peas, and saw the old woman lying on the ground in such a battered condition that he scarcely knew her, and of his grandchildren there was no trace. The grandfather cried aloud, picked up the old woman, dragged her home by degrees, gradually brought her to with a little cold water, and she opened her eyes at last and told the grandfather who it was that had beaten her so, and dragged her grandchildren away from the field. The grandfather was very wroth with Verlioka, and said: "This is too much of a joke! Wait a bit, friend, we also have arms of our own! Look to thyself, Verlioka, and take care that I don't twist thy moustaches for thee! Thou hast done this thing with thy hand, thou shalt pay for it with thy head!" And as the old grandmother did not hold him back, the grandfather seized his iron crutch and went off to seek Verlioka.

He went on and on till he came to a little pond, and in the pond was swimming a bob-tailed drake. He saw the grandfather and cried: "'Tak, tak, tak![1] Live for a hundred years, old grandad! I have been

[1] So, so, so.

waiting here for thee a long time!"—"Hail to thee also, drake! Why hast thou been awaiting me?"—"Well I know that thou art in quest of thy grandchildren, and art going to Verlioka to settle accounts with him!"—"And how dost thou come to know of this monster?"—"Tak, tak, tak!" screeched the drake, "I have good cause to know him, 'twas he who docked my tail!"—"Then canst thou show me his dwelling?"—"Tak, tak, tak!" screeched the drake; "here am I but a little tiny bird, but I'll have my tail's worth out of him, I know!"—"Wilt thou go on before and show me the way? I see thou hast a good noddle of thy own, though thou art bob-tailed!" Then the drake came out of the water and climbed up on the bank, waddling from side to side.

They went on and on, and they came upon a little bit of cord lying in the road, and it said, "Hail, little grandad wise-pate!"—"Hail, little cord!"—"Where dost thou dwell, and whither dost thou wander?"—"I live in such and such a place; I am going to pay off Verlioka; he has beaten my old woman and carried off my two grandchildren, and such splendid grandchildren too!"—"Take me that I may help!" The grandfather thought: "I may as well take it, it will do to hang Verlioka with." Then he said to the little cord: "Come along with us, if thou dost know the way." And the little cord wriggled after them just as if it were a little tapering snake.

They went on and on, and they saw lying in the road a little water-mill, and it said to them: "Hail, little grandad wise-pate!"—"Hail, little water-mill!"—"Where dost thou dwell, and whither dost thou wander?"—"I live in such and such a place, and I am going to settle accounts with Verlioka. Just fancy! he has beaten my old woman and carried off my grandchildren, and such splendid grandchildren too!"—"Take me with thee that I may help!" And the grandfather thought: "The water-mill may be of use too." Then the water-mill raised itself up, pressed against the ground with its handle, and went along after the grandfather.

Again they went on and on, and in the road lay an acorn, and it said to them in a little squeaky voice: "Hail, grandad long-nose!"—"Hail, oakey acorn!"—"Whither art thou striding away like that?"—"I am going to beat Verlioka; dost know him?"—"I should think I did; take me with thee to help!"—"But how canst thou help?"—"Don't spit in the well or thou wilt have to drink up the water thyself!" The grandfather thought to himself: "I may as well let him go!" So he said to the acorn: "Roll on behind then!" But that was a strange rolling, for the acorn leaped to its feet and frisked along in front of them all.

And they came into a thick forest, a forest most drear and dreadful, and in the forest stood a lonely little hut—oh! so lonely. There was no fire burning in the stove, and there stood there a furmenty-pottage for six. The acorn, who knew what he was about, immediately leaped into the pottage, the little cord stretched itself out on the threshold, the grandfather placed the little water-mill on the bench, the drake sat upon the stove, and the grandfather himself stood in the corner. Suddenly he heard a crashing and a trembling in the wood, and Verlioka came along on one leg, in a wooden boot, leaning on his crutch and smiling from ear to ear. Verlioka came up to the hut, threw down some fire-wood on the floor, and began to light the fire in the stove. But the acorn who was sitting in the pottage fell a-singing—

"Pee, pee, pee!
To beat Verlioka come we!"

Verlioka flew into a rage and seized the pot by the handle, but the handle broke, and all the pottage was scattered over the floor, and the acorn leaped out of the pot and flipped Verlioka in his one eye so that it was put out entirely. Verlioka fell a-shrieking, fought about the air with his arms, and would have made for the door; but where was the door? he could not see it! Then the little cord wound itself about his legs and he fell on the threshold, and the little water-mill on the top of him off the bench. Then the grandfather rushed out of the corner and pitched into him with his iron crutch, and the drake on the top of the stove screeched with all its might: "Tak, tak, tak! Pitch into him! pitch into him!" Neither his wrath nor his strength was of any good to Verlioka. The grandfather beat him to death with his iron crutch, and after that, destroyed his hut and laid bare the dungeon beneath it; and out of the dungeon he drew his grandchildren, and dragged all Verlioka's riches home to his old woman. And so he lived and prospered with his old woman and his grandchildren, and plucked and ate his peas in peace and quietness. So there's a skazka[1] for you—and I deserve a cake or two also.

[1] Fairy-tale.

THE FROG-TSAREVNA.

In a certain kingdom, in a certain Empire, there lived a Tsar with his Tsaritsa, and he had three sons, all of them young, valiant, and unwedded, the like of whom is not to be told in tales nor written by pens, and the youngest of them was called the Tsarevich Ivan. And the Tsar spoke these words to them: "My dear children, take unto you your darts, gird on your well-spanned bows, and go hence in different directions, and in whatsoever courts your arrows fall, there choose ye your brides!" The elder brother discharged his arrow and it fell into a boyar's[1] court, right in front of the *terem*[2] of the maidens. The second brother discharged his arrow, and it flew into the court of a merchant and remained sticking in a beautiful balcony, and on this balcony was standing a lovely young maiden soul, the merchant's daughter. The youngest brother discharged his arrow, and the

[1] Nobleman.   [2] The women's apartments.

arrow fell in a muddy swamp, and a quacking-frog seized hold of it.

The Tsarevich Ivan said to his father: "How can I ever take this quacker to wife? A quacker is not my equal!"—"Take her!" replied his father, "'tis thy fate to have her!" So the Tsareviches all got married—the eldest to the boyar's daughter, the second to the merchant's daughter, and the youngest to the quacking-frog. And the Tsar called them to him and said: "Let your wives, to-morrow morning, bake me soft white bread." The Tsarevich Ivan returned home, and he was not happy, and his impetuous head hung down lower than his shoulders. "Qua, qua! Ivan the Tsarevich! wherefore art thou so sad?" asked the Frog. "Or hast thou heard unpleasant words from thy·father the Tsar?"— "Why should I not be sad? my father and sovereign lord hath commanded thee to bake soft white bread to-morrow."—"Do not afflict thyself, O Tsarevich! lie down and rest, the morning is wiser than the evening." She made the Tsarevich lie down and rest, cast her frog-skin, and turned into a maiden soul, Vasilisa Premudraya,[1] went out upon her beautiful balcony, and cried with a piercing voice: "Nurseys —nurseys! assemble, set to work and make me soft white bread such as I myself used to eat at my dear

[1] Super-sapient cross-gentian.

father's!" In the morning the Tsarevich Ivan awoke, the frog had got the bread ready long ago, and it was so splendid that the like of it is neither to be imagined nor guessed at, but is only to be told of in tales. The loaves were adorned with various cunning devices, royal cities were modelled on the sides thereof, with moats and ditches. The Tsar praised the Tsarevich Ivan greatly because of his bread, and gave this command to his three sons: "Let your wives weave me a carpet in a single night." The Tsarevich Ivan returned home, and he was sad, and his impetuous head hung lower than his shoulders. "Qua! qua! Tsarevich Ivan! wherefore art thou so sad? Or hast thou heard cruel, unfriendly words from thy father the Tsar?"—"Have I not cause to grieve? My father and sovereign lord commands thee to weave him a silk carpet in a single night!"—"Fret not, Tsarevich! come, lay thee down and sleep, the morning is wiser than the evening!" Then she made him lie down to sleep, threw off her frog-skin, and turned into the lovely maiden soul, Vasilisa Premudraya, went forth upon her beautiful balcony, and cried with a piercing voice: "Nurseys—nurseys! assemble, set to work and weave me a silk carpet such as I was wont to sit upon at my dear father's!" No sooner said than done. In the morning the Tsarevich Ivan awoke, and the frog had had the carpet ready long ago, and it was such a wondrous carpet that the like of it can only be told of in tales, but may neither be imagined nor guessed at. The carpet was adorned with gold and silver and with divers bright embroiderings. The Tsar greatly praised the Tsarevich Ivan for his carpet, and there and then gave the new command that all three Tsareviches were to appear before him on the morrow to be inspected together with their wives. Again the Tsarevich Ivan returned home and he was not happy, and his impetuous head hung lower than his shoulders. "Qua! qua! Tsarevich Ivan! wherefore art thou grieved? Or hast thou heard words unkind from thy father the Tsar?"—"Have I not cause to be sad? My father and sovereign lord has commanded me to appear before him with thee to-morrow! How can I show thee to people?"—"Fret not, Tsarevich! Go alone to the Tsar and pay thy visit, and I will come after thee. The moment you hear a rumbling and a knocking, say: 'Hither comes my dear little Froggy in her little basket!'" And behold the elder brothers appeared, to be inspected with their richly-attired and splendidly-adorned consorts. There they stood and laughed at the Tsarevich Ivan and said: "Why, brother! why hast thou come hither without thy wife? Why thou mightest have brought her with thee in a kitchen clout. And where didst thou pick up such a beauty? I suppose thou didst search through all the swamps fairly?" Suddenly there was a great rumbling and knocking, the whole palace shook. The guests were all terribly frightened and rushed from their places, and knew not what to do with themselves, but the Tsarevich Ivan said: "Fear not, gentlemen! 'tis only my little Froggy coming in her little basket!" And then a golden coach drawn by six horses flew up to the steps of the Tsar's balcony, and out of it stepped Vasilisa Premudraya; such a beauty as is only to be told of in tales, but can neither be imagined nor guessed at. The Tsarevich Ivan took her by the hand and led her behind the oaken table, behind the embroidered table-cloth. The guests began to eat and drink and make merry. Vasilisa Premudraya drank wine, but the dregs of her cup she poured behind her left sleeve; she ate also of the roast swan, but the bones thereof she concealed behind her right sleeve. The wives of the elder brothers watched these devices, and took care to do the same. Afterwards when Vasilisa Premudraya began dancing with the Tsarevich Ivan, she waved her left hand and a lake appeared; she waved her right hand and white swans were swimming in the water; the Tsar and his guests were astonished. And now the elder brides began dancing. They waved their left hands and all the guests were squirted with water; they waved their right hands and the bones flew right into the Tsar's eyes. The Tsar was wroth, and drove them from court with dishonour.

Now one day the Tsarevich Ivan waited his opportunity, ran off home, found the frog-skin, and threw it into a great fire. Vasilisa Premudraya duly arrived, missed her frog-skin, was sore troubled, fell a-weeping, and said to the Tsarevich: "Alas! Tsarevich Ivan! what hast thou done? If thou hadst but waited for a little, I should have been thine for ever more, but now farewell! Seek for me beyond lands thrice-nine, in the Empire of Thrice-ten, at the house of Koshchei Bezsmertny."[1] Then she turned into a white swan and flew out of the window.

The Tsarevich Ivan wept bitterly, turned to all four points of the compass and prayed to God, and went straight before his eyes. He went on and on, whether it was near or far, or long or short, matters not, when there met him an old, old man. "Hail, good youth!" said he, "what dost thou seek, and whither art thou going?" The Tsarevich told him all his misfortune. "Alas! Tsarevich Ivan, why didst thou burn that frog-skin? Thou didst not make, nor shouldst thou therefore have done away with it. Vasilisa Premudraya was born wiser and more cunning than her father; he was therefore

[1] The deathless skeleton.

angry with her, and bade her be a frog for three years. Here is a little ball for thee, follow it whithersoever it rolls." Ivan the Tsarevich thanked the old man, and followed after the ball. He went along the open plain, and there met him a bear. "Come now!" thought the Tsarevich Ivan, "I will slay this beast." But the bear implored him: "Slay me not, Tsarevich Ivan, I may perchance be of service to thee somehow." He went on further, and lo! behind them came waddling a duck. The Tsarevich bent his bow; he would have shot the bird, when suddenly she greeted him with a human voice: "Slay me not, Ivan Tsarevich! I also may befriend thee!" He had compassion on her, and went on further, and a hare darted across their path. The Tsarevich again laid an arrow on his bow and took aim, but the hare greeted him with a human voice: "Slay me not, Tsarevich Ivan! I also will befriend thee!" Ivan the Tsarevich had pity upon him, and went on further to the blue sea, and behold! on the beach lay gasping a pike. "Alas! Tsarevich Ivan!" sighed the pike, "have pity on me and cast me into the sea." And he cast it into the sea, and went on along the shore. The ball rolled a short way, and it rolled a long way, and at last it came to a miserable hut; the hut was standing on hen's legs and turning round and round. The Tsarevich Ivan said to it: "Little hut, little hut! stand the old way as thy mother placed thee, with thy front to me, and thy back to the sea!" And the little hut turned round with its front to him, and its back to the sea. The Tsarevich entered in, and saw the bony-legged Baba-Yaga lying on the stove, on nine bricks, and grinding her teeth.—"Hillo! good youth, why dost thou visit me?" asked the Baba-Yaga.—"Fie, thou old hag! thou call'st me a good youth, but thou shouldst first feed and give me to drink, and prepare me a bath, then only shouldst thou ask me questions." The Baba-Yaga fed him and gave him to drink, and made ready a bath for him, and the Tsarevich told her he was seeking his wife, Vasilisa Premudraya. "I know," said the Baba-Yaga, "she is now with Koshchei Bezsmertny. 'Tis hard to get thither, and it is not easy to settle accounts with Koshchei. His death depends upon the point of a needle, that needle is in a hare, that hare is in a coffer, that coffer is on the top of a high oak, and Koshchei guards that tree as the apple of his eye." The Baba-Yaga then showed him in what place that oak grew; the Tsarevich Ivan went thither, but did not know what to do to get at the coffer. Suddenly, how who can tell, the bear rushed at the tree and tore it up by the roots, the coffer fell and was smashed to pieces, the hare leaped out, and with one bound had taken cover. But look!

the other hare bounded off in pursuit, hunted him down and tore him to bits; out of the hare flew a duck and rose high, high in the air, but the other duck dashed after her, and struck her down, whereupon the duck laid an egg, and the egg fell into the sea. The Tsarevich Ivan, seeing the irreparable loss of the egg, burst into tears, when suddenly the pike came swimming ashore holding the egg between its teeth. He took the egg, broke it, drew out the needle and broke off its little point. Then he attacked Koshchei, who struggled hard, but wriggle about as he might he had to die at last. Then the Tsarevich Ivan went into the house of Koshchei, took out Vasilisa Premudraya, and returned home. After that they lived together for a long, long time, and were very, very happy.

THE TWO SONS OF IVAN THE SOLDIER.

THERE once dwelt in a certain kingdom a peasant. The time came when they enlisted him as a soldier; he had to quit his wife, and as he bade her good-bye, he said to her, "Hearken, wife! live honestly; flout not good people; do not let our little hut fall to pieces, but keep house wisely, and await my return. If God permit it, I will come back and leave the service. Here are fifty rubles!—whether a little son or a little daughter be born to thee matters not; keep the money till the child grows up. If it be a daughter, wed her to the bridegroom whom God may provide; but if God give thee a son, and he arrive at years of discretion, this money will be of no little help to him." Then he took leave of his wife, and went to the wars whither he was bidden. Three months passed, and the wife gave birth to twin sons, and she called them the sons of Ivan the soldier. The youngsters grew up betimes; like wheaten dough mixed with yeast they shot up broad and high. When they reached their tenth year their mother gave them instruction, and they quickly learned their letters, and the children of the boyars and the children of the merchants could not hold a candle to them; no one could read aloud, or write, or answer questions so well as they. The two sons of Ivan the soldier thus grew up, and they asked their mother, "Mother, dear! did not our father leave us some money? If there be any, let us have it, and we'll take it to the fair and buy us a good horse apiece." Their mother gave them the fifty rubles, twenty-five to each brother, and said to them, "Hearken, children, as ye go to the town, give a bow to every one you come across."—"Good, dear mother."

So the brothers hied them off to the town, and went to the horse-market. There were many horses there, but they chose none of them, for they were not good enough mounts for the good brothers. So one of the brothers said to the other: "Let us go to the other end of the square; look how the people are all running together there. There is something strange going on." Thither they went and joined the crowd; and there stood two mares tied to stout oaken posts with iron clamps; one with six clamps, and the other with twelve clamps. The horses were tugging at their chains, gnawing their bits, and digging up the ground with their hoofs. No one was able to go near them. "What is the price of thy mares?" asked Ivan, the soldier's son, of the owner. "Don't thrust thy nose in here, friend!—such mares are not for the like of thee. Ask no more about them!"—"How dost thou know what I am? Maybe I'll buy them, but I must first look at their teeth." The horse-dealer smiled: "Look out for your heads, that's all!" One of the brothers then drew near to the mare that was fastened by six clamps, and the other brother to the mare that was fastened by twelve. They tried to look at the horses' teeth, but how was it to be done? The mares rose on their hind legs and pawed the air. Then the brothers struck them in the breast with their knees; the chains which held the horses burst, and the mares flew up into the air five fathoms high, and fell down with their legs uppermost. "Well!" cried the brothers, "that's not much to boast of. We would not take such horses at a gift." The crowd cried "Oh!" and was amazed. "What strong and stalwart heroes are these?" The horse-dealer was almost in tears. The mares galloped all over the town, and made off over the wide steppe; nobody dared approach them, and nobody knew how to catch them. The sons of Ivan the soldier were sorry for the horse-dealer. They went out into the open steppe, cried with a piercing

voice and whistled lustily, and the mares came
running back and stood in their proper place as if
they had been nailed there. Then the good youths
put the iron chains upon them again, and tied them
to the oaken posts, and bound them tightly. This
they did, and then they went homewards. As they
were going along there met them an old graybeard.
They forgot what their mother had told them, and
passed him by without greeting him. Suddenly one
of them recollected himself and cried: " Oh, brother!
what have we done? We never gave that old man
a bow; let us run after him and bow to him!" They
ran after the old man, took off their little caps, bowed
to the very girdle, and said, " Forgive us, dear little
father, for passing thee by without a greeting. Our
mother straitly charged us to pay honour to every
one we met in the way."—"Thanks, good youths!
whither is God leading you?"—" We have been to
the town fair; we wanted to buy us a good horse
apiece, but there are none there which please us."
—" Why, how's that? Suppose now that I were to
give you a little nag apiece?"—" Ah! little father,
we would then always pray to God for thee!"—
" Well, come with me."—The old man led them to
a huge mountain, opened two cast-iron doors, and
brought out two horses of heroic breed. " Here,
take your horses and depart in God's name, good

youths, and may ye prosper with them!" They thanked him, mounted and galloped home; reached the courtyard, bound their horses to a post, and entered the hut. Their mother then began, and asked them: "Well, my dear children, have you bought yourselves a little nag apiece?"—"We have not bought them with money, but got them as a gift."—"Where have you left them?"—"We put them beside the hut."—"Alas! my children, look if any one has taken them away."—"Nay, dear mother, such horses are not taken away. No one could lead them, and there's no getting near them!" The mother went out, looked at the horses, and burst into tears. "Well, my dear sons, ye are surely never those whom I have nourished."

The next day the sons begged their mother to let them go into the town to buy them a sword apiece. "Go, my children!" Then they got them ready, went to the smith's, entered the master's house, and said: "Make us a couple of swords!"—"Why should I make them when they are ready made? Take whichever you like best."—"No, friend, we want swords which weigh ten puds[1] each."—"What are you thinking of? Who would be able to wield a machine like that? You'll find such swords nowhere." So there was nothing for the good youths to do but

[1] Four hundred pounds.

return homewards with hanging heads. As they were on their way the same old man met them again. "Hail, young men!"—"Hail, dear little father!"—"Whence do you come?"—"From town, from the smith's. We wanted to buy two Damascus blades, and there were none that suited our hands."— "How stupid! Suppose now I were to give you a sword apiece?"—"Ah, dear little father, in that case we would pray to God for thee for evermore." The old man led them to the huge mountain, opened the cast-iron door, and drew out two heroic swords. The brothers took them, thanked the old man, and their hearts were merry and joyful. They came home, and their mother asked them: "Well, my children, have you bought yourselves a sword a-piece?"—"We have not bought them for money, but got them as a gift."—"And what have you done with them?"—"We have placed them beside the hut."—"Take care lest some one take them away."—"Nay, dear mother, nobody will take them away, for it is impossible to even carry them." The mother went out into the courtyard and looked; the two heavy, heroic swords were leaning against the wall, the hut was scarce able to bear the weight of them. The old woman burst into tears and said: "Well, my dear sons, ye are surely never those whom I have nourished."

The next morning the sons of Ivan the soldier saddled their good horses, took their heroic blades, went into the hut, prayed to God, and took leave of the mother who bore them. "Bless us, dear little mother, for a long journey is before us."—"My irremovable, motherly blessing be upon you. Go, in God's name. Show yourselves, and see the world. Offend none without cause, and follow not evil ways."—"Be not afraid, dear mother; our motto is, 'When I eat I don't whistle, and when I bite I don't let go.'" Then the good youths mounted their horses and rode off. Whither they went, near or far, long or short, the tale is soon told, but the deed is not soon done; anyhow, they came to a cross-way where stood two pillars. On one pillar was written, "Who goes to the right will become a Tsar," and on the other pillar was written, "Who goes to the left will become a corpse." The brothers stood still, read the inscriptions, and fell a-thinking. "Whichever way shall we go? If we both go to the right, there will not be honour and glory enough for the heroic strength and youthful prowess of us both; but nobody wants to go to the left and die." And one brother said to the other: "Look now, dear brother, I am stronger than thou; let me go a little on the left to see how death can get hold of me. But thou go to the right, and perchance God will make thee a Tsar." Then they took leave of each other, and each gave to the other a little piece of cloth, and they made this compact—each was to go his own way and place posts along the road, and write on these posts everything concerning himself as a mark and guide; every morning each of them was to wipe his face with his brother's cloth, and if blood appeared on the cloth it would mean that death had befallen his brother, and in such a calamity he was to hasten back to seek his dead. So the good youths parted in different directions. He who turned his horse to the right came to a splendid kingdom. In this kingdom dwelt a Tsar and his Tsaritsa, and they had a daughter called the thrice-beautiful Tsarevna Nastasia. The Tsar beheld the son of the soldier Ivan, loved him for his knightly valour, and without beating about the bush, gave him his daughter as a consort, called him the Tsarevich Ivan, and bade him rule over the whole kingdom. The Tsarevich Ivan lived right merrily, loved his wife dearly, gave good laws to his kingdom, and diverted himself with the pleasures of the chase.

But his brother, Ivan the soldier's son, who had taken the road to the left, went on day and night without rest. A month, and a second month, and a third passed by, and he found himself in an unknown empire, in the midst of the capital. In this empire there was great mourning, the houses were covered with black cloth, and the people crept about as if they were dreaming. He hired him a lodging at a poor old woman's, and began to ask her, "Tell me, old mother, why are all the people in this empire of thine so full of woe, and all the houses covered with black cloth?"—"Alas, good youth! a great grief weighs upon us; every day there comes out of the blue sea, from beyond the gray rock, a twelve-headed serpent and eats up a man every time, and now it has come to the turn of the Tsar's own house. He has three most lovely Tsarevnas; at this very time they are escorting the youngest of them to the sea-shore to be devoured by the monster." Ivan the soldier's son mounted his horse and rode off to the blue sea, to the gray rock; on the shore stood the thrice-lovely Tsarevna, tied to an iron chain. She saw the hero and said to him, "Depart hence, good youth. The twelve-headed serpent will soon be here; I shall perish, nor wilt thou escape death; the cruel serpent will devour thee also." "Fear not, lovely maiden. Perhaps it may be overcome." And Ivan the soldier's son went up to her, burst the chain with his heroic hand, and broke it into little bits as if it were rotten rope; then he lit a large fire all round the rock and nourished it with the trunks of uprooted oaks and pines, piled them up into a huge pyre, and then went back to the lovely maiden, laid his head on her knee, and said to her, "I must rest, but thou look seawards, and as soon as a cloud arises, and the wind begins to blow, and the sea to leap and roar, awaken me, young maiden." So he spake, and fell into a deep sleep, and the lovely maiden watched over him, and sat and looked out upon the sea. Suddenly a cloud rose above the horizon, and the wind began to blow, and the sea to leap and roar; the serpent was coming forth from the blue sea, and raised itself mountains high. The Tsarevna tried to awake Ivan the soldier's son; she shook him and shook him; it was of no use, he heard her not; then she burst into tears, and her burning tear-drops fell upon his cheeks. At this the hero awoke, ran to his horse, and the good horse had already ploughed up half a fathom of earth with his hoofs. The twelve-headed serpent rushed straight at him, belching forth fire; it looked upon the hero and cried, "Goodly art thou and comely, fair youth, but thy last hour has come. Say farewell to the wide world, and gallop down my throat as quickly as thou canst." —"Thou liest, cursed serpent; surrender!" Then they fell to mortal combat. Ivan the soldier's son struck so deftly and sturdily with his sword that it grew red-hot, there was no holding it in his hand. Then he cried to the Tsarevna: "Save me, lovely maiden! Take out thy fair kerchief, dip it in the blue sea, and wrap it round my sword." The Tsarevna immediately moistened her kerchief in the sea, and gave it to the good youth. He wrapped it round his sword and again fell fiercely on the serpent, but he found that he could not despatch the serpent with his sword. Then he snatched a burning pine-brand from the pyre and burnt out the serpent's eye, and then he hewed off all its twelve heads, placed them beneath the rock, cast the body into the sea, and then trotted home, ate and drank, and laid him down to sleep for thrice four-and-twenty hours.

And in the meantime the Tsar called his water-carrier and said to him: "Go to the sea-shore and collect the bones of the Tsarevna, if haply ye find them." The water-carrier went down to the sea-shore, and lo! the Tsarevna was in no way hurt. He placed her on the cart and drove her into the drear forest— far into the forest he drove her—drew his knife from his girdle, and began to sharpen it. "What art thou doing?" asked the Tsarevna. "I am sharpening my knife. I mean to slay thee. Tell thy father that I slew the serpent, and I'll have mercy on thee." He terrified the lovely maiden, and she took an oath to speak according to his words. Now this daughter was the Tsar's favourite, and when the Tsar saw that she was alive, and in no way hurt, he wished to reward the water-carrier, and gave him his youngest daughter to wife; and the rumour of it went through the whole realm. Ivan the soldier's son heard also that a marriage was being celebrated at the Tsar's, and straight to court he went. There a great banquet was proceeding; the guests were eating and drinking, and diverting themselves with divers pastimes. The youngest Tsarevna looked at Ivan the soldier's son, and saw his sword wrapped round with her costly kerchief, whereupon she leaped from her chair, seized his hand, and cried: "My dear father and sovereign lord, lo! here is he who saved us from the cruel serpent and from violent death. The water-carrier can only sharpen his knife and say—'I am sharpening my knife. I mean to kill thee.'" The Tsar was wroth, and he bade them hang the water-carrier, and gave the Tsarevna to Ivan the soldier's son as his consort, and there was great rejoicing. And the young couple lived together, and their life was happy and prosperous.

Not a very long time passed away, and then this thing befell the Tsarevich Ivan, the other son of Ivan the soldier.

One day he was going a-hunting, and he started a swift-footed stag. The Tsarevich Ivan put spurs to his horse and pursued the stag. On and on he sped, and he came to a vast meadow. Here the stag vanished from before his eyes. Ivan looked about him and considered—" Whither does my way lie now ?" And, lo, in that meadow a little stream was flowing, and on the water two gray ducks were swimming. He took aim at them, fired, and slew the ducks, dragged them out of the water, put them into his knapsack, and went on further. He went on and on till he saw a palace of white stone, dismounted from his horse, fastened it to a post, and went into the rooms. They were all empty, not a living soul was to be seen, only in one room was there a lighted stove, a pan for a meal of six stood there, and the table was already laid ; there were plates and glasses and knives. The Tsarevich Ivan pulled the ducks from his pocket and drew them, put them in the pan, cooked them, placed them on the table, and began carving and eating them. Suddenly, whence I know not, a lovely damsel appeared to him, so lovely that the like of her cannot be told of in tales or written with pens, and she said to him : " Bread and salt, Ivan the Tsarevich."—" I cry thy pardon, lovely damsel, sit down and eat with me."—" I would sit down with thee, but I am afraid. Thou hast an enchanted horse."—" Nay, lovely damsel, thou art ill-informed. I have left my magic horse at home, and am riding on a common one." No sooner did the lovely damsel hear this than she began to swell out and swell out till she became a frightful lioness, opened wide her jaws, and swallowed up the Tsarevich Ivan whole. She was not an ordinary damsel, but the very sister of the serpent who had been slain by Ivan the soldier's son.

And it fell about this time that the other Tsarevich Ivan bethought him of his brother, drew his kerchief out of his pocket, dried his face with it, and saw that the whole kerchief was covered with blood. Sorely grieved was he. "What's the matter?" he cried. He took leave of his wife and father-in-law, and went forth on his heroic horse to seek his brother. He went near and far, and long and short, and at last he came to the same realm where his brother had lived. He asked about everything, and learnt that the Tsarevich had indeed gone hunting and disappeared—not a trace of him could be found. Ivan went a-hunting the selfsame way, and there met him a swift-footed stag. The hero pursued after it; he came out into the vast meadow, and the stag vanished from before his eyes. In the meadow he saw a little stream flowing, and two gray ducks were swimming on the water. Ivan the soldier's son shot the ducks, came to the white stone palace, and went into the rooms. They were all empty, only in one room was a stove lighted and a pan for a meal for six was upon it. He roasted the ducks, went out into the courtyard, sat on the steps, and began carving them up and eating. Suddenly a lovely damsel appeared before him. "Bread and salt, good youth, why dost thou eat in the courtyard?" Ivan the soldier's son answered: "In the rooms it is not to my mind; in the courtyard 'twill be more pleasant. Sit down with me, fair damsel!"— "I would sit down gladly, but I fear thy enchanted horse."—"No need, damsel. I am riding on an ordinary nag." Like a fool she believed him, and began to swell out, and swelled into a frightful lioness, and would have swallowed up the good youth, when his magic horse ran up and seized her round the body with its heroic feet. Ivan the soldier's son drew his sharp sword and cried with a piercing voice: "Stand, accursed one. Hast thou not swallowed my brother, the Tsarevich Ivan? Give him back to me, or I'll cut thee into little bits." The red lioness turned back again into a most lovely damsel, and began to beg and pray: "Spare me, good youth. Take the two phials from that bench full of healing and living water, follow me into the underground chamber, and revive thy brother."

The Tsarevich Ivan followed the lovely damsel into the underground chamber, and saw his brother lying there torn to bits. He sprinkled his brother with the healing water, the flesh and fat grew together again.

He sprinkled him with the living water, and his brother stood up and spoke: "Ah! how long have I slept?" Ivan the Tsarevich said, "Thou wouldst have slept for ever but for me." And the brothers returned to court, made a three days' feast, and then took leave of each other. Ivan the soldier's son remained with his wife, and lived with her in love and harmony and enduring bliss. But the Tsarevich returned to his realm, and I met him on his way; three days he drank and diverted himself with me, and 'twas he who told me all this tale.

THE WOMAN-ACCUSER.

THERE was once upon a time an old man and an old woman. The old woman was not a bad old woman, but there was this one bad thing about her—she did not know how to hold her tongue. Whatever she might hear from her husband, or whatever might happen at home, she was sure to spread it over the whole village; she even doubled everything in the telling, and so things were told which never happened at all. Not unfrequently the old man had to chastise the old woman, and her back paid for the faults of her tongue.

One day the old man went into the forest for wood. He had just got to the border of the forest, when his foot, in treading on a certain place, sank right into the ground. "Why, what's this?" thought the old man. "Come, now, I'll dig a bit here; maybe I shall be lucky enough to dig out something." He dug several times, and saw, buried in the ground, a little cauldron quite full of silver and gold. "Look, now, what good luck has befallen me! But what am I to do with it? I cannot hide it from that good wife of mine at home, and she will be sure to blab to all the world about my lucky find, and thou wilt repent the day thou didst ever see it."

For a long time the old man sat brooding over his treasure, and at last he made up his mind what to do. He buried the treasure, threw a lot of wood over it, and went to town. There he bought at the bazaar a live pike and a live hare, returned to the wood, and hung the pike upon a tree, at the very top of it, and carried the hare to the stream, where he had a fish-basket, and he put the hare into it in a shallow place.

Then he went off home, whipped up his little nag for pure lightness of heart, and so entered his hut. "Wife, wife," he cried, "such a piece of luck has befallen me that I cannot describe it!"—"What is it, what is it, hubby darling? Why dost thou not tell me?"—"What's the good, when thou wilt only blab it all about?"—"On my word, I'll say nothing to anybody. I swear it. I'll take the holy image from the wall and kiss it if thou dost not believe me."—"Well, well, all right. Listen, old woman!" and he bent down towards her ear and whispered, "I have found in the wood a cauldron full of silver and gold."—"Then why didst thou not bring it hither?"—"Because we had both better go together, and so bring it home." And the old man went with his old woman to the forest.

They went along the road, and the peasant said to his wife, "From what I hear, old woman, and from what people told me the other day, it would seem that fish are now to be found growing on trees, while the beasts of the forest live in the water."—"Why, what art thou thinking about, little hubby? People nowadays are much given to lying."—"Lying, dost thou call it? Then come and see for thyself." And he pointed to the tree where the pike was hanging. "Why, what marvel is this?" screamed the old woman. "However did that pike get there? Or have the people been speaking the truth to thee after all?" But the peasant stood there, and moved his arms about, and shrugged his shoulders, and shook his head, as if he could not believe his own eyes. "Why dost thou keep standing there?" said the old woman. "Go up the tree, rather, and take the pike; 'twill do for supper." So the peasant took the pike, and then they went on further. They passed by the stream, and the peasant stopped his horse. But his wife began screeching at him, and said, "What art gaping at now? let us make haste and go on."— "Nay, but look! I see something struggling about all

round my fish-basket. I'll go and see what it is."
So he ran, looked into the fish-basket, and called to
his wife. "Just come and look here, old woman!
Why, a hare has got into our fishing-basket!"—
"Then people must have told thee the truth after all.
Fetch it out quickly; it will do for dinner on the
feast-day." The old man took up the hare, and then
went straight towards the treasure. He pitched away
the wood, digged wide and deep, dragged the cauldron
out of the earth, and they took it home.

The old man and the old woman grew rich, they
lived right merrily, and the old woman did not
improve; she went to invite guests every day, and
gave such banquets that she nearly drove her husband
out of the house. The old man tried to correct her.
"What's come to thee?" he cried "Canst thou not
listen to me?"—"Don't order me about," said she.
"I found the treasure as well as thou, and have as
much right to make merry with it." The old man
put up with it for a very long time, but at last he
said to the old woman straight out, "Do as best thou
canst, but I'm not going to give thee any more money
to cast to the winds." But the old woman immediately fell foul of him. "I see what thou art up to,"
screeched she; "thou wouldst keep all the money
for thyself. No, thou rogue, I'll drive thee whither
the crows will pick thy bones. Thou wilt have no

good from thy money." The old man would have chastised her, but the old woman thrust him aside, and went straight to the magistrate to lay a complaint against her husband. "I have come to throw myself on thy honour's compassion, and to present my petition against my good-for-nothing husband. Ever since he found that treasure there is no living with him. Work he won't, and he spends all his time in drinking and gadding about. Take away all his gold from him, father. What a vile thing is gold when it ruins a man so!" The magistrate was sorry for the old woman, and he sent his eldest clerk to him, and bade him judge between the husband and wife. The clerk assembled all the village elders, and went to the peasant and said to him, "The magistrate has sent me to thee, and bids thee deliver up all thy treasure into my hands." The peasant only shrugged his shoulders. "What treasure?" said he. "I know nothing whatever about any treasure."—"Not know? Why, thy old woman has just been to complain to the magistrate, and I tell thee what, friend, if thou deniest it, 'twill be worse for thee. If thou dost not give up the whole treasure to the magistrate, thou must give an account of thyself for daring to search for treasures, and not revealing them to the authorities."—"But I cry your pardon, honoured sirs! what *is* this treasure you are talking of? My wife must have seen this treasure in her sleep; she has told you a pack of nonsense, and you listen to her."—"Nonsense!" burst forth the old woman; "it is not nonsense, but a whole cauldron full of gold and silver!"—"Thou art out of thy senses, dear wife. Honoured sirs, I cry your pardon. Cross-examine her thoroughly about the affair, and if she proves this thing against me, I will answer for it with all my goods."—"And dost thou think that I cannot prove it against thee? Thou rascal, I will prove it. This is how the matter went, Mr. Clerk," began the old woman; "I remember it, every bit. We went to the forest, and we saw a pike on a tree."—"A pike?" roared the clerk at the old woman; "or dost thou want to make a fool of me?"—"Nay, I am not making a fool of thee, Mr. Clerk; I am speaking the simple truth."—"There, honoured sirs," said the old man, "how can you believe her if she goes on talking such rubbish?"—"I am not talking rubbish, yokel! I am speaking the truth—or hast thou forgotten how we found a hare in thy fishing-basket in the stream?"—All the elders rolled about for laughter; even the clerk smiled, and began to stroke down his long beard. The peasant again said to his wife, "Recollect thyself, old woman; dost thou not see that every one is laughing at thee? But ye, honoured gentlemen, can now see for yourselves how far you can believe my wife."—"Yes," cried all the elders, with one voice, "long as we have lived in the world, we have never heard of hares living in rivers, and fish hanging on the trees of the forest." The clerk himself saw that this was a matter he could not get to the bottom of, so he dismissed the assembly with a wave of his hand, and went off to town to the magistrate.

And everybody laughed so much at the old woman that she was forced to bite her own tongue and listen to her husband; and the husband bought wares with his treasure, went to live in the town, and began to trade there, exchanged his wares for money, grew rich and prosperous, and was as happy as the day was long.

THOMAS BERENNIKOV.

ONCE upon a time there lived in a village a miserably poor peasant called Tommy Berennikov. Thomas's tongue could wag right well, and in mother-wit he was no worse than his neighbours, but he was anything but handsome to look at, and for working in the fields he was not worth a button. One day he went into the field to plough. The work was heavy and his nag was a wretched hack, quite starved and scarce able to drag along the plough, so at last Tom quite gave way to woe, sat down on a little stone, and immediately whole swarms of blow-flies and gad-flies fell upon his poor knacker from every quarter and stuck fast. Thomas seized a bundle of dry twigs and thwacked his horse about the back with all his might; the horse never stirred from the spot, and the blow-flies and gad-flies fell off him in swarms. Thomas began to count how many he had killed, eight gad-flies, and there was no numbering the slain of the other flies. And Thomas Berennikov smiled. "That's something like!" said he, "we've killed eight at a blow! And there's no counting the smaller fry! What a warrior I am, what a hero! I won't plough any more, I'll fight. I'll turn hero, and so seek my fortune!" And he took his crooked sickle from his shoulders, hung up his bast-basket by his girdle, placed in this basket his blunt scythe, and then he mounted his hack and wandered forth into the wide world.

He went on and on till he came to a post on which passing heroes had inscribed their names, and he wrote with chalk on this post, "The hero Thomas Berennikov has passed by this way, who slew eight at one blow, and of the smaller fry without number." This he wrote and went on further. He had only got a mile from this post when two stalwart young heroes came galloping up to it, read the inscription, and asked one another, "What unheard-of hero is this? Whither has he gone? I never heard of his gallant steed, and there is no trace of his knightly deed!" They followed hard upon Thomas, overtook him, and were amazed at the sight of him. "What sort of a horse is the fellow riding on?" cried they; "why, 'tis a mere hack! Then all this prowess cannot be in the horse, but in the hero himself." And they both rode up to Thomas and said to him quite humbly and mildly, " Peace be with thee, good man." Thomas looked at them over his shoulder, and without moving his head, said, " Who are you ? "—" Ilia Muromets and Alesha Popovich ; we would fain be thy comrades."—" Well, maybe you'll do. Follow behind me pray."

They came to the realm of the neighbouring Tsar and went straight into his preserves ; here they let their horses out to graze, and laid themselves down to rest beneath their tent. The neighbouring Tsar sent out against them a hundred horsemen of his guard, and bade them drive away the strangers from his preserves. Ilia Muromets and Alesha Popovich said to Thomas, " Wilt thou go against them, or wilt thou send us ? "—" What, forsooth ! do you think I'd soil my hands by going against such muck ! No ; go thou, Ilia Muromets, and show thy prowess." So Ilia Muromets sat him on his heroic steed, charged the Tsar's horsemen, swooped down upon them like a bright falcon on a flock of doves, smote them, and cut them all down to the very last one. At this the Tsar was still more wroth, collected all of his host that was in the town, both horse and foot, and bade his captains drive the wandering strangers out of his preserves without ceremony. The Tsar's army advanced on the preserves, blew with their trumpets, and columns of dust arose in their path. Ilia

Muromets and Alesha Popovich came to Thomas and said to him, "Wilt thou go thyself against the foe, or wilt thou send one of us?" But Thomas, who was lying on his side, did not so much as turn him round, but said to the heroes, "The idea of my coming to blows with this rabble!—the idea of my soiling my heroic hands with the like of them! No! Go thou, Alesha Popovich, and show them our style of fighting, and I'll look on and see if thy valour be of the right sort." Alesha rushed like a whirlwind upon the Tsar's host, his armour rattled like thunder, he waved his mace from afar, and shouted with a voice more piercing than the clang of clarions, "I will slay and smash all of you without mercy!" He flew upon the host and began crushing it. The captains saw that every one took to his heels before him, and there was no way of stopping them, so they blew a retreat with the trumpets, retired towards the town, and came themselves with an apology to Alesha, and said: "Tell us now, strong and potent hero, by what name we must call thee, and tell us thy father's name that we may honour it. What tribute must we give thee that thou mayst trouble us no more, and leave our realm in peace?"—"'Tis not to me you must give tribute!" answered Alesha; "I am but a subordinate. I do what I am bidden by my elder brother, the famous hero Thomas Berennikov. You must reckon with him. He will spare you if he pleases, but if he does not please, he will level your whole kingdom with the ground." The Tsar heard these words, and sent Tommy rich gifts and an honourable embassy of distinguished persons, and bade them say: "We beg the famous hero Thomas Berennikov to come and visit us, to dwell in our royal court, and help us to war against the Khan of China. If, O hero, thou dost succeed in smiting utterly the countless Chinese host, then I will give thee my own daughter, and after my death thou shalt have the whole realm." But Tommy put on a long face and said, "What's that? Well, well, I don't mind! I suppose I may as well consent to that." Then he mounted his hack, commanded his heroic younger brethren to ride behind him, and went as a guest to the neighbouring Tsar.

Tommy had not yet thoroughly succeeded in testing the quality of the Tsar's kitchen, he had not yet thoroughly rested from his labours, when there came a threatening embassy from the Khan of China, demanding that the whole kingdom should acknowledge him as its liege lord, and that the Tsar should send him his only daughter. "Tell your Khan," replied the Tsar, "that I fear him no longer; I now have a firm support, a sure defence, the famous hero Thomas Berennikov, who can slay eight at one blow of his sword, and of the lesser fry without number. If life is not pleasant to your Khan and your Chinese brethren, come to my empire, and you shall have cause to remember Thomas Berennikov." In two days a countless Chinese host surrounded the city of the Tsar, and the Chinese Khan sent to say, " I have here an unconquerable hero, the like of whom the world knows not; send out against him thy Thomas. If thy champion prevails I'll submit and pay thee a tribute from my whole Khanate; but if mine prevails, thou must give me thy daughter, and pay me a tribute from thy whole kingdom." So now it was the turn of Thomas Berennikov to show his prowess ! And his heroic younger brothers, Ilia Muromets and Alesha Popovich, said to him: " Mighty and potent hero, our elder brother, how wilt thou fight against this Chinaman without armour? Take our martial armour, choose the best of our heroic horses!" Thomas Berennikov answered thus: " How then? Must I hide myself in armour from this shaven pate? Why, I could finish off this Chinaman with one hand quite easily! Why, you yourselves when you first saw me said, 'Tis plain that we must not look at the horse, but at the warrior!" But Thomas thought to himself: "I'm in a pretty pickle now! Well, let the Chinaman kill me if he likes—I'll not be put to shame over the business anyhow!" Then they brought him his hack: he mounted it in peasant style, struck it with his bunch of twigs, and went into the open plain at a gentle amble.

The Chinese Khan had armed his champion like a fortress; he clothed him in armour twelve puds (480 lbs.) in weight, taught him the use of every weapon, put in his hands a battle-axe eighty pounds in weight, and said to him just before he set out, "Mark me, and recollect my words! When a Russian hero cannot prevail by force, he will overcome by cunning, so lest thou should get the worst of it, take care and do everything the Russian hero does." So the champions went out against each other into the open field, and Thomas saw the Chinese hero advancing against him, as big as a mountain, with his head like a beer-cask, and covered with armour like a tortoise in its shell, so that he was scarcely able to move. So Tommy had recourse to artifice. He got off his horse and sat down on a stone and began to sharpen his scythe. The Chinese hero when he saw that, got off his horse immediately, fastened it to a tree, and began to whet his axe against a stone also. When Thomas had finished sharpening his scythe, he marched up to the Chinaman and said to him, "We two are mighty and potent heroes, we have come out against each other in mortal combat; but before we pitch into each other we ought to show each other proper respect, and salute one another after the custom of the country." And he saluted the Chinaman with a low, a very low bow. "Oh, oh!" thought the Chinaman, "here's some piece of trickery, I know. I'll bow yet lower." And he bowed himself to the very ground. But before he could raise himself up again in his heavy armour, Thomas rushed at him, tickled him once or twice in the neck, and so cut his throat through for him. Then he leaped upon the heroic horse of the Chinaman, scrambled on the top of it somehow, flourished his birch of twigs, tried to grasp the reins, and quite forgot that the horse was tied to a tree. But the good horse, as soon as he felt a rider on his back, tugged and pulled till he tore the tree up by the roots, and off he set at full gallop towards the Chinese host, dragging after him the big tree as if it had been a mere feather. Thomas Berennikov was terribly frightened, and began bawling, "Help, help!" But the Chinese host feared him more than a snowstorm, and it seemed to them as if he were crying to them, "Run, run!" so they took to their heels without once looking back. But the heroic horse plunged into the midst of them, trampled them beneath its feet, and the huge tree-trunk scattered them in all directions. Wherever it plunged it left a wide road behind it.

The Chinese swore that they would never fight

with Thomas again, and this resolution was lucky for Thomas. He returned to the town on his own hack, and they were all amazed at his strength, valour, and success. "What dost thou require of me?" said the Tsar to Thomas, "one half of my golden treasures and my daughter into the bargain, or one half of my glorious kingdom?" "Well, I'll take half your kingdom if you like, but I wouldn't turn up my nose either at your daughter with half your golden treasure for a dowry. And look now, when I get married, don't forget to invite to the wedding my younger brothers, Ilia Muromets and Alesha Popovich!"

And Thomas married the thrice-lovely Tsarevna, and they celebrated the wedding so gloriously that the heads of all the guests ached for more than two weeks afterwards. I too was there, and I drank mead and ale and got rich gifts, and so my tale is told.

THE WHITE DUCK.

A POWERFUL and mighty Prince married a thrice-lovely Princess, and he had not yet had time to look upon her, he had not yet had time to speak to her, he had not yet had time to listen to her, when he was obliged to depart from her on a far journey, and leave his young wife in the hands of strangers. The Princess wept much, and the consolations of the Prince were also many, and he advised her not to leave her lofty terem,[1] not to have anything to do with bad people, not to listen to evil tongues, and not to consort with strange women. All this the Princess promised to do. The Prince departed, and she shut herself up in her own room. There she sat, and never went out.

Whether it was after a long time or after a short time matters not, but one day she was sitting by her little window, bathed in tears, when a woman passed by the window. In appearance she was simple and

[1] The women's apartments.

kindly, and she leaned her elbows on her crutch, rested her chin on her hands, and said to the Princess in a wheedling, caressing voice: "How's this, darling little Princess, thou art for ever fretting? Prythee come now out of thy terem and have a peep at God's fair world, or come down into thy little garden among the sweet green things and drive away thy woe!" For a long time the Princess refused, she did not even care to listen to the woman's words, but, at last, she thought, "There can be no harm in going into the garden, crossing the brook is another matter." But she did not know that this woman was a witch, and had come to ruin her because she envied her her bliss. So the Princess went with her into the garden, and listened to her cunning, wheedling words. And in the garden from beneath the mountain trickled a stream of crystalline water. "What dost thou say now," said the woman, "the day is very hot, the sun is burning with all its might, but this darling little stream is so cold, so refreshing, and hark how it babbles—why should we not have a bath here?" "Ah, no, no! I won't," said the Princess; but she thought to herself, "But why not? There can be no harm in having a bath!" So she slipped off her little sarafan,[1] and bounded into the water, and no sooner had she bathed than the witch struck her on the

---

[1] A long, sleeveless upper garment.

The Princess and the cunning Witch.

P. 160.

P. 160.

shoulder and said, "Swim about now as a white duck!" But the witch immediately dressed herself in the Princess's robes, tired and painted herself, and sat in place of the Princess in the terem to await the Prince. And as soon as the little dog began to bark and the little bell fell a-tinkling, she rushed out to meet him, threw herself upon his neck, and kissed and fondled him. The Prince was so overjoyed that he was the first to stretch out his arms towards her, and never noticed that it was not his wife, but an evil witch who stood before him.

Meanwhile the poor duck, dwelling in the bright stream, laid eggs and hatched its young; two were fair, but the third was still-born, and her babies grew up into little children. She brought them up, and they began to walk along the stream, and catch goldfish, and collect bits of rags, and sew them coats, and run up the banks, and look at the meadows. But the mother said: "Oh! don't go there, my children. There dwells the evil witch. She ruined me, and she will ruin you!" But the children didn't listen to their mother, and one day they played in the grass, and the next day they ran after ants, and went further and further, and so got into the Prince's courtyard. The witch knew them by instinct, and ground her teeth for rage; but she made herself so nice, called the little children into the out-house, gave them a good feed, and a good drink, and made them lie down to sleep, and bade her people light a fire in the courtyard, and put a kettle on it, and sharpen their knives. The two brothers went to sleep, but the still-born one whom the mother had bade the others carry in their bosom that he might not catch cold, the still-born one did not sleep at all, but listened and saw everything. In the night the witch came to their door and said: "Are you asleep, little children, or not?" Then the still-born one answered instead of his brothers: "We do not dream in dreams, but think in our thoughts that you want to cut up the whole lot of us!—the pyres of maple-branches are blazing, the kettles are seething, and the knives of steel are sharpening."—"They are not asleep," said the witch, and she went away from the door, walked about and walked about, and then went to the door again: "Are you asleep, children, or are you not?" And the still-born again screeched from beneath the pillow instead of his brethren: "We do not dream in dreams, but think in our thoughts that you want to cut up the whole lot of us; the pyres of maple-branches are blazing, the kettles are seething, and the knives of steel are sharpening." "How is it that it is always one and the same voice?" thought the witch; "I'll just have a peep." She opened the door very, very softly, looked in, and saw both the brothers sleeping soundly. Then she killed the pair of them.

THE WHITE DUCK.

In the morning the white duck began seeking and calling her children, but her darling children did not come to her calling. Her heart had a foreboding of evil. She shuddered and flew off to the Prince's courtyard. In the Prince's courtyard, as white as little white kerchiefs, as cold as little cold split fish, lay the brothers all in a row. She flew down, threw herself upon them, fluttered her little wings, flew round and round her little ones, and cried with a mother's voice:

> "Kra, kra, my darling loveys!
> Kra, kra, my little doveys!
> I brought you up in woe and fears,
> I nourished you with grief and tears,
> Dark night it brought no sleep to me,
> No food was sweet because of ye."

And the Prince heard the lament, called the witch to him, and said: "Wife, hast thou heard this thing, this thing unheard of?"—"Thou dost only fancy it! Hi! my serving-men, drive me this duck out of the courtyard!" They began driving her out, but she flew round and round, and again said to her children:

> "Kra, kra, my darling loveys!
> Kra, kra, my little doveys!
> The old, old witch your bane hath been,
> The old, old witch, that cruel snake,
> That cruel snake that lurks unseen;
> Your father from you she did take,

> Your father dear, my husband true;
> Us in the running stream she threw.
> She changed us into ducks so white,
> And prospers as if wrong were right!"

The Prince felt that there was something wrong here, and he cried: "Bring me that white duck hither!" They all hastened to fulfil his command, but the white duck flew round in a circle, and none could catch her. At last the Prince himself went out on the balcony, and she flew upon his hands, and fell at his feet. The Prince took her carefully by her little wing, and said: "White birch-tree stand behind me, and fair damsel stand before me!" Then the white duck turned into her former shape of thrice-lovely Princess, taught them how to get a little bladder of living and speaking water in a magpie's nest, sprinkled her children with the living water, and they shuddered; then she sprinkled them with the speaking water, and they began to speak. And the Prince suddenly saw himself surrounded by his family all alive and well, and they all lived together, and lived happily, and chose good and avoided evil.

But the witch, by the Prince's command, was fastened to the tail of a horse and dragged away over the open steppe. The fowls of the air picked her flesh, and the wild winds of heaven scattered her bones, and there remained not a trace or a memorial of her behind.

THE TALE OF LITTLE FOOL IVAN.

FAR, far away, in a certain kingdom, in a certain Empire, stood a city, and in this city reigned Tsar Gorokh,[1] and the Tsaritsa Morkovya.[2] They had many wise Boyars, rich Princes, strong and mighty heroes, and of the common run of warriors 100,000 at least. All manner of people dwelt in this city, worshipful, well-bearded merchants, cunning open-handed sharpers, German mechanics, Swedish beauties, drunken Russians; and in the suburbs beyond the town dwelt peasants who tilled the earth, sowed corn, ground it into meal, took it to the bazaar, and drank away their hard earnings.

In one of these suburbs stood an old hut, and in this hut dwelt an old man with his three sons, Pakhom, Thomas, and Ivan. The old man was not only sage, he was cunning, and whenever he chanced to come across the Devil, he would have a chat with

[1] Pea.   [2] Carrot.

him, make him drunk, and worm many and great secrets out of him, and then would go away and do such wonders that his neighbours called him a wizard and a magician, while others honoured him as a shrewd fellow who knew a thing or two. The old man certainly did great wonders. If any one were being consumed by the flames of hopeless love, he had only to pay his respects to the wizard and the old man would give him some sort of little root which would draw the fickle fair one at once. If anything were lost he would manage to get it back from the thief, however it might be hidden, by means of charmed water and a fishing-net.

But wise as the old man was, he could not persuade his sons to walk in his footsteps. Two of them were great gad-abroads, not because they were wise, but because they were thorough feather-brains; they never knew when to run forward or when to hold back. And they married and had children. The third son was not married, but the old man did not trouble about him, because his third son was a fool, quite a natural in fact, who couldn't count up to three, but could only eat and drink and sleep and lie on the stove. What was the good of bothering about a fellow like that?— he can manage to jog along of his own accord much better than a man of sense. And besides, Ivan was so mild and gentle that butter would not melt in his mouth. If you asked him for his girdle, he would give you his kaftan[1] also; if you took away his gloves, he would beg you to accept his cap into the bargain; therefore they all liked Ivan and called him dear little Ivan, or dear little fool; in short he was a fool from his birth, but very lovable for all that.

So our old man lived and lived with his sons till the hour came when he was to die. Then the old man called to him his three sons and said to them: "My dear children, my mortal hour has come, and you must fulfil my wish; each of you must come with me into my tomb and there pass a night with me; thou first, Thomas; then thou, Pakhom; and thou third, dear little fool Ivan." The two elders, like sensible people, promised to obey his words, but the fool promised nothing, but only scratched his head.

The old man died. They buried him. They ate pancakes and honey-cakes, they drank well, and on the first night it was for his eldest son Thomas to go into his tomb. Whether it was laziness or fear I know not, but he said to little fool Ivan: "To-morrow I have to get up early to grind corn; go thou instead of me into our father's tomb."—"All right!" answered little fool Ivan, who took a crust of bread, went to the tomb, lay down, and began to snore. So it

[1] Coat.

struck midnight, the tomb began to move, the wind blew, the midnight owl hooted, the tombstone rolled off, and the old man came out of his tomb and said: "Who's there?"—"I," answered little fool Ivan.—"Good!" answered the old man; "my dear son, I'll reward thee for obeying me!" Scarcely had he said these words when the cocks crew and the old man fell back into the tomb. Little fool Ivan went home and threw himself on the top of the stove, and his brother asked him: "Well, what happened?"—"Nothing at all!" said he; "I slept the whole night through, only I am very hungry, and want something to eat."

The next night it was the turn of Pakhom, the second son, to go to the tomb of his father. He fell a-thinking and a-thinking, and at last he said to little fool Ivan: "I must get up very early to-morrow morning to go to market; go thou instead of me to my father's tomb."—"All right!" replied little fool Ivan, who took a cake and some cabbage-soup, went to the tomb, and lay down to sleep. Midnight approached—the tomb began to shake, the tempest began to howl, a flock of ravens flew round and round it, the stone fell from the grave, the old man got out of the tomb and asked: "Who's there?"—"I," answered little fool Ivan.—"Good, my beloved son!" replied the old man, "I'll not forget thee because thou hast not disobeyed me!" Scarcely had he uttered these words when the cocks began to crow, and the old man fell back in his tomb. Little fool Ivan awoke, made himself snug on his stove, and his brother asked him: "Well, what happened?"—"Nothing at all!" answered little Ivan. On the third night the brothers said to little fool Ivan: "Now 'tis thy turn to go to our father's tomb. A father's wish must be fulfilled." —"By all means!" answered little fool Ivan, who took a fritter, put on his blouse, and went to the tomb. And at midnight the gravestone was torn from the tomb, and the old man came out and asked: "Who's there?"—"I," said little fool Ivan. "Good, my obedient son," answered the old man, "not in vain hast thou obeyed my will—thou shalt have a reward for thy faithful service!" And then he shouted with a monstrous voice and sang with a nightingale's piping voice: "Hi! thou! sivka-burka, vyeshchy kaurka[1]! Stand before me like the leaf before the grass!" And it seemed to little fool Ivan as if a horse were running, the earth trembled beneath it, its eyes burned like fire, clouds of smoke poured out of its ears; it ran up, stood still as though it had taken root in the ground, and said with a human voice: "What dost thou require?" The old man got into one of its ears, cooled himself, washed

[1] Grizzled, dark-brown, red-brown, knowing steed.

himself, dressed himself finely, and came out of the other ear so young and handsome that there's no guessing or imagining it, for no pen can write nor tale can tell the like of it. "There, my dear son," said he, "thou hast my valiant steed; and thou, O horse! my good steed, serve him as thou hast served me!" He had scarcely uttered these words when the crowing cocks of the village flapped their wings and sang their morning song, the magician sank back into his grave, and the grass grew over it. Little fool Ivan went home step by step; he got home, stretched himself in his old corner, and snored till the walls trembled. "What is it?" asked his brothers, but he never answered a word, but only waved his hand.

And so they went on living together, the elder brothers like wise men, the younger like a fool. Thus they lived on and on, day by day, and just as a woman rolls thread into a ball, so their days rolled on till it came to their turn to be rolled. And one day they heard that the captains of the host were going all about the realm with trumpets and clarions and drums and cymbals, and they blew their trumpets and beat their drums, and proclaimed in the bazaars and public places the Tsar's will, and the will of the Tsar was this. Tsar Gorokh and Tsaritsa Morkovya had an only daughter, the Tsarevna Baktriana, the heir to the throne, and so lovely that when she looked at the sun, the sun was ashamed, and when she regarded the moon, the moon was abashed. And the Tsar and the Tsaritsa thought to themselves: To whom shall we give our daughter in marriage that he may govern our realm, defend it in war, sit as judge in the royal council, help the Tsar in his old age, and succeed him at the end of his days? The Tsar and the Tsaritsa sought for a bridegroom who was to be a valiant young warrior, a handsome hero, who was to love the Tsarevna, and make the Tsarevna love him. But the love part of the business was not so easy, for there was this great difficulty: the Tsarevna loved nobody. If her father the Tsar began talking to her of any bridegroom, she always gave one and the same answer: "I don't love him!" If her mother the Tsaritsa began talking to her about any one, she always answered: "He is not nice!" At last Tsar Gorokh and Tsaritsa Morkovya said to her: "Dear daughter and darling child, more than thrice lovely Tsarevna Baktriana, it is now time for thee to choose a bridegroom. Look now, pray! the wooers, the royal and imperial ambassadors, are all here at our court; they have eaten all the cakes and drained our cellars dry, and still thou wilt not choose thee the beloved of thy heart!" Then the Tsarevna said to them: "My sovereign papa and my sovereign mamma, I am sorry for your sorrow, and would feign obey your will, but let fate decide who is to be my intended. Build me a terem[1] thirty-two storeys high with a little bow-window at the top of it. I, the Tsarevna, will sit in this terem just beneath the window, and you make a proclamation. Let all people come hither—Tsars, Kings, Tsareviches, Princes, mighty champions, and valiant youths; and whoever leaps up as high as my little window on his fiery steed and exchanges rings with me, he shall be my bridegroom, and your son and successor." The Tsar and the Tsaritsa followed out the words of their sage daughter. "Good!" said they. They commanded to be built a costly terem of two-and-thirty layers of oak beams; they built it up and adorned it with curious carvings, and hung it all about with Venetian brocade, with pearly tapestries and cloth of gold, and made proclamations and sent forth carrier-pigeons, and despatched ambassadors to all kingdoms, summoning all men to assemble together in the empire of Tsar Gorokh and Tsaritsa Morkovya, and whoever leaped on his proud steed as high as the two-and-thirty oaken beams and exchanged rings with the Tsarevna Baktriana, he was to be her bridegroom and inherit the kingdom with her, whether he were a Tsar or a King, or a Tsarevich or a Prince, or even nothing but a free, bold-handed Cossack with neither birth nor ancestry.

[1] The women's apartments in old Russian houses.

The day was fixed. The people crowded into the meadows where the Tsarevna's terem was built as if sewn with stars, and the Tsarevna herself sat beneath the window arrayed in pearls and brocade, and lace, and the most precious of precious stones. The mob of people surged and roared like the great sea Ocean. The Tsar and the Tsaritsa sat on their throne, and around them stood their grandees, their Boyars, their captains, and their heroes. And the wooers of the Tsarevna Baktriana came and pranced and galloped, but when they saw the terem their hearts died away within them. The youths tried their best; they ran, they bounded, they leaped, and fell back on the ground again like sheaves of barley, to the amusement of the crowd.

In those days when the valiant wooers of the Tsarevna Baktriana were trying their best to win her, the brothers of little fool Ivan took it into their heads to go thither and see the fun. So they got them ready, and little fool Ivan said: "Take me with you too!"—"What, fool!" answered his brother; "sit at home and look after the fowls! What hast thou got to do with it!"—"You're right!" said he, and he went to the fowl-house and lay down there. But when his brethren had departed, little fool Ivan went into the open plain, on to the wide steppe, cried with a warrior's voice, and whistled with a heroic whistle:

"Hi! thou! sivka-burka, vyeshchy kaurka! Stand before me like the leaf before the grass!" And lo! the valiant charger came running up, the earth trembled, flames shot out of his eyes, and clouds of smoke from his ears, and it said with a human voice: "How can I serve thee?" Little fool Ivan crept into one ear, washed and combed himself, and crept out of the other ear so young and handsome, that books cannot describe it, nor the eye of man bear the sight of it. And he sat him on his good horse, and struck its sturdy ribs with a whip of Samarcand silk, and his horse chafed and fumed, and rose from the earth higher than the standing woods, but lower than the moving clouds, and when it came to the large streams it swam them, and when it came to the little streams it brushed them away with its tail, and opened wide its legs for the mountains to pass between them. And little fool Ivan leaped up to the terem of the Tsarevna Baktriana, rose like a bright falcon, leaped over thirty of the two-and-thirty beams of oak, and dashed along like a passing tempest. The people roared: "Hold him, stop him!" The Tsar leaped up, the Tsaritsa cried "Oh!" the people were astonished.

The brothers of little fool Ivan returned home and said to each other: "That was something like a hero; he only missed two storeys." "Why, that was I, brothers!" said little fool Ivan. "Thou indeed! Hold thy tongue, fool, and lie on the stove and eat cinder cakes!"

The next day the brothers of little fool Ivan again assembled at the Tsar's sports, and little fool Ivan said to them: "Take me with you!"—"Take thee, fool!" said the brothers; "just sit at home and keep the sparrows from the peas instead of a scarecrow! What hast thou to do with it!"—"That's true!" said he, went among the peas, sat down, and scared away the sparrows. But when his brothers had gone, little fool Ivan shuffled off into the open plain, into the wide steppe, and roared with a martial voice, and whistled shrilly with a heroic whistle: "Hi! thou! sivka-burka, vyeshchy kaurka! Stand before me like the leaf before the grass!" And lo! his valiant steed came running, the earth trembled, sparks flew from beneath his prancing hoofs, a fire burned in his eyes, and smoke rolled in clouds from his ears. He said with a human voice: "What dost thou require?" Little fool Ivan crept into one of the horse's ears, and crept out of the other so young and comely that the like of it was never heard of in tales or seen in reality, and he sat on his brave horse and beat its iron ribs with a Circassian whip. And his horse chafed and fumed, and rose from the earth, higher than the standing woods, lower than the moving clouds; at one bound it went a league of the ancient measure; at the second bound it whizzed across the broad river; and at the third bound it reached the terem. It rose into the air like an eagle into the sky, leaped as high as thirty-one of the two-and-thirty oaken beams, and flew past like a passing whirlwind. The people cried: "Hold him, stop him!" The Tsar leaped from his seat, the Tsaritsa cried "Oh!" The Princes and the Boyars stood there with gaping mouths.

The brothers of little fool Ivan returned home and said to each other: "Why, that young warrior of to-day was even better than the warrior of yesterday; there was only one oak beam he could not get as high as!"—"Why, brothers, that was I!" said little fool Ivan.—"Hold thy tongue! Thou indeed! Lie on the stove, and don't talk bosh!"

On the third day the brothers of little fool Ivan again made them ready to go to the great spectacle, but little fool Ivan said: "Take me with you!"—"A fool like thee!" replied his brethren; "just stay at home and mix the slush in the trough for the pigs. What art thou thinking of!"—"As you please!" said he, and went into the backyard, and began to feed the swine, and grunt along with them. But when his brothers had gone, little fool Ivan shambled off to the open plain, to the wide steppe, and howled with a martial voice, and whistled as only heroes can whistle: "Hi! thou! sivka-burka, vyeshchy kaurka! Stand before me like the leaf before the grass!" And lo! the valiant charger came running, the earth trembled; where it touched the ground with its foot springs gushed forth, and where it struck the ground with its hoof lakes appeared, and flames came from its eyes, and clouds of smoke welled from its ears. It cried with a human voice: "What dost thou require?" Little fool Ivan crept into one of his horse's ears, and crept out of the other a youthful warrior, so handsome that no lovely maiden ever dreamed the like of him in her dreams, and a hundred sages meditating for a hundred years could not have imagined it. He struck his horse on the backbone, drew tight the rein, sat in the saddle, and rushed away so swiftly that the fleeting wind could not overtake him, and the dear little house-swallow would not vie with him. He flew like a cloud of the sky, his silver harness hissed and gleamed, his yellow locks floated in the wind; he flew towards the Tsarevna's terem, struck his horse about the ribs, and his horse leaped like a cruel serpent, and leaped as high as the two-and-thirty oaken beams. Little fool Ivan caught the Tsarevna Baktriana in his heroic hands, kissed her sugary lips, exchanged rings with her, and was borne as by a whirlwind into the meadow, overturning all that met him or stood in his way. The

Tsarevna only just succeeded in fastening a diamond star on his forehead—and the mighty warrior had vanished. Tsar Gorokh leaped to his feet, the Tsaritsa Morkòvya said "Oh!" The Tsar's councillors wrung their hands one after another, but spake never a word.

The brothers of little fool Ivan returned home and began to talk about and discuss the matter: "Well, the hero of to-day was the best of all; he is now the bridegroom of our Tsarevna. But who is he?"—"Why, brothers, it was I," said little fool Ivan.—"Hold thy tongue! Thou indeed! Go and eat cinder cakes and toad-stools, but keep thy tongue well between thy teeth!" But Tsar Gorokh commanded them to surround the city with a strong watch, and let in every one, but let out no one, and proclaim that all people, under pain of death, from the eldest to the youngest, were to come into the Tsar's courts and do homage, that it might appear on whose forehead was the diamond star which the Tsarevna had fastened to her bridegroom. From very early in the morning the people came crowding together. They looked at everybody's forehead, but there was no star, and no trace of a star. It was now dinner-time, yet not a single table in the halls of the Tsar was yet laid for dinner. The brothers of little fool Ivan also came thither to show their foreheads at the Tsar's command, and Ivan said to them: "Take me with you!"—"Take thee!" said the brothers; "sit in thy corner and catch flies! But why hast thou tied thy forehead round with rags, or hast thou damaged it?"—"Yesterday, when you went out, as I was gaping about, I struck my forehead against the door, the door took no hurt, but a big lump sprang out on my forehead!" As soon as his brothers had gone, little fool Ivan passed right below the little window where the Tsarevna was sitting troubled at heart. The soldiers of the Tsar saw him, and asked: "Why hast thou bound up thy forehead? Show it! Is there not a star on thy forehead?" Little fool Ivan would not let them look, and withstood them. The soldiers began to make a to-do, the Tsarevna heard it, and bade them bring little fool Ivan to her, took the clouts from his forehead—and behold! there was the star. She took little fool Ivan by the hand, led him to Tsar Gorokh, and said: "Look, dear sovereign papa! this is my intended bridegroom, and thy son-in-law and successor!" There was nothing more to be said. The Tsar commanded the banquet to be made ready; they married little fool Ivan and the Tsarevna Baktriana; for three days they ate and drank and made merry, and amused themselves with all manner of amusements. The Tsar made the brothers of little fool Ivan captains of his host, and gave them a village and a large house apiece.

The tale of it is soon told, but the deed thereof is not soon done. The brethren of little fool Ivan were wise, and when they grew rich it is not strange that all men gave them out for wise men at once. And when the brethren of little fool Ivan became great people, they began to be proud and haughty, would not suffer men of low degree to come into their courtyards at all, and made even the old voevods and Boyars, when they came to see them, take off their caps on the stairs. So the Boyars came to Tsar Gorokh and said: "Sovereign Tsar! the brethren of thy son-in-law boast that they know where the apple tree grows that hath silver leaves and golden apples, and they want to get this apple tree for thee!" The Tsar sent for the brethren of little fool Ivan, and told them that they might fetch for him this apple tree with the silver leaves and the golden apples; and as they had nothing to say they were obliged to go. The Tsar bade them take horses from the royal stables for their journey, and they set out on their journey to find the apple tree with the silver leaves and the golden apples. And in those days little fool Ivan arose, took his old hack of a horse, sat on it with his face to the tail, and rode out of the city. He went into the open plain, seized his jade by the tail, threw it into the open field, and said: "Come, ye crows and kites, here's a breakfast for you!" Then he called his good horse, crept in at one ear and out at the other, and his horse carried him to the East where grew the apple tree with silver leaves and golden apples, on the silver waters, by the golden sands, and he pulled it up by the roots, went back, and before he got to the town of Tsar Gorokh, he pitched his tent with its silver tent-pole and laid him down to rest. Now his brethren were going along by this road, their noses hung down, and they did not know what to say to the Tsar by way of excuse, and they saw the tent and the apple tree beside it, and they awoke little fool Ivan, and they began to bargain with him for it, and offered him three cart-loads of silver. "The apple tree is mine, gentlemen; it was not sold and purchased, but bequeathed by will," said little fool Ivan to them. "Yet a will is no great matter: cut off a toe from the right foot of each one of you, and I'll say done!" The brothers laid their heads together, but there was nothing for it but to agree. So little fool Ivan cut off one of their toes apiece and gave them the apple tree, and they brought it to the Tsar and boasted mightily. "Behold, O Tsar!" said they, "we have travelled far, we have suffered many hardships, but we have performed thy will." Tsar Gorokh was overjoyed. He made a great feast, bade them beat the drums, and play on the trumpets and pipes, and he rewarded the brothers of little fool Ivan, and gave them a city apiece, and praised their faithful service.

Then the other voevods and Boyars said to him: "It is not a very great service to bring the apple tree with silver leaves and golden apples. The brothers of thy son-in-law boast that they would go to the Caucasus and fetch thee the swine with golden bristles, and silver teeth, and twenty sucking-pigs." Tsar Gorokh sent for the brothers of little fool Ivan, and told them to bring him the swine with the golden bristles, and the silver teeth, and the twenty sucklings; and as they had nothing to say for themselves, they dared not disobey. So they went on their way to find for the Tsar's pleasure the little pig with the golden bristles, and the silver teeth, and the twenty sucklings. And at that very time little fool Ivan arose and saddled his cow, and sat upon it with his face to the tail, and went out of the city. He went into the open plain, seized his cow by the horn, threw her into the field, and cried: "Gallop along, ye gray wolves and pretty little foxes! Here's a dinner for you!" Then he called his good horse, and crept in at one ear and out at the other, and his horse bore him to lands of the South, and bore him into a dreary wood where the little swine with the golden bristles was rooting up roots with its silver tusks, and twenty sucking-pigs were running after her. Little fool Ivan threw a silk lasso over the little swine, strapped the sucklings to his saddle, turned back, and when he was not very far from the city of Gorokh, pitched his tent with the golden tent-pole, and lay down to rest. Now his brothers were coming along that same way, and were thinking what they could say to the Tsar. Suddenly they saw the tent, and close by it tied by the silken lasso the little swine with the golden bristles, and the silver tusks, and the twenty sucklings. They awoke little fool Ivan, and began to bargain with him for the swine. "We'll give thee three sacks of precious stones," they cried. "The little swine is mine, gentlemen," said little Ivan the fool; "it is not sold or purchased, but bequeathed by will; but a will is no great matter; let each of you cut me off a finger from his hand, and I'll cry done!" The brothers laid their heads together and talked the matter over: "People can live without brains, why not without fingers also?" thought they. So they let little fool Ivan cut off a finger from each of them, and he gave them the swine, which they took to the Tsar, and they praised themselves more than ever. "Tsar!" said they, "we have been beyond the distant sea, beyond the impenetrable woods, beyond the shifting sands; we have suffered cold and hunger, but we have fulfilled thy commands." The Tsar was overjoyed to have such faithful servants, gave a great banquet to all the world, rewarded the brethren of little fool Ivan, made them great Boyars, and could not praise their services sufficiently.

Then the other voevods and Boyars came to him and said: "'Tis not such a very great service, O Tsar! to bring thee the little swine with the golden bristles, and the silver tusks, and the twenty sucklings. A swine's a swine all the world over, though it has got golden tusks! But the brethren of thy son-in-law boast that they can do a yet greater service; they say they can get thee from the stables of the Serpent Goruinich,[1] the golden-maned horse with the diamond hoofs." Tsar Gorokh sent for the brethren of little fool Ivan, and bade them fetch him from the stables of the Serpent Goruinich, the golden-maned mare with the diamond hoofs. Then the brothers of little fool Ivan began protesting that they had never said such words. But the Tsar would not listen to a word of it. "Take of my treasures without tale or count," said he, "and of my host as much as you will. Bring me hither the golden-maned mare. Ye are the first in my realm, but if you bring her not, I will again degrade you into ragamuffins." So these good warriors, these useful heroes, departed, scarce able to drag one foot after another, and not knowing whither they were going. And in the self-same time little fool Ivan arose, sat astride his little

[1] Dweller in the mountains.

stick, went out into the open plain, into the wide steppe, called his good horse, crept into one ear and out at the other, and his horse took him into the west country, towards the great island where the Serpent Goruinich guarded in his iron stable, behind seven bolts, behind seven doors, the golden-maned mare with the diamond hoofs. The horse went on and on, near and far, high and low, and little fool Ivan arrived at the island, fought three days with the Serpent till he killed it, spent three days more in bursting the locks and breaking the doors, took out the golden-maned mare by the mane, went back, and had not gone many miles when he stopped, pitched his tent with the diamond tent-pole, and laid him down to rest. And behold his brethren were coming along by the same way, and knew not what they should say to Tsar Gorokh. All at once they felt the ground tremble—'twas the neighing of the golden-maned mare! They looked about them, and there was a little light like a candle burning in the dark distance—'twas the golden mane which burned like fire. They stopped, awoke little fool Ivan, and began to bargain with him for the mare; they said they would each give him a sack of precious stones. "The mare is mine, gentlemen, 'tis not for purchase or sale, but was bequeathed by will," said little fool Ivan. "However, a will is not such a great matter; let each of you cut him an ear off, and

I'll cry done!" The brothers did not say him nay, but they let little fool Ivan cut off an ear from each one of them, and he gave them the mare with the golden mane and the diamond hoofs, and they puffed themselves out and talked big, and lied boastingly till it made your ears ache to hear them. "We went," said they to the Tsar, "beyond lands thrice-ten, beyond the great sea Ocean, we strove with the Serpent Goruinich, and look! he bit off our ears, but for thy sake we reck not of life or goods, but would swim through rivers of blood, and would sacrifice limb and substance in thy service." In his joy Tsar Gorokh measured them out riches without number, made them the first of his Boyars, and got ready such a feast that the royal kitchens were not big enough for it, though they cooked and roasted there three days, while the royal wine-cellars ran dry, and at the banquet Tsar Gorokh placed one of the brethren of little fool Ivan at his right hand, and the other at his left. And the feast proceeded right merrily, and the guests had eaten themselves half full, and drank themselves half full, and were humming and buzzing like bees in a hive, when they saw entering the palace a gallant warrior, little fool Ivan, in just the same guise as when he had leaped as high as the two-and-thirty oaken beams. And when his brothers saw him, one of them nearly choked himself with a drop of wine from his beaker, and the other nearly suffocated himself with a bit of roast swan, and they wrung their hands, rolled their eyes, and could not utter a word. Little fool Ivan bowed low to his father-in-law, the Tsar, and told how he had got the apple tree with the silver leaves and the golden apples, and after that the swine with the golden bristles and the silver tusks and the twenty sucklings, and after that the golden-maned mare with the diamond hoofs; and he drew out the fingers, and the toes, and the ears for which he had sold them to his brethren.

Then Tsar Gorokh was very wroth, and stamped with his feet, and bade them drive out the brothers of little fool Ivan with broomsticks, and one of them he sent to tend his swine in the cattle-yard, and the other he sent to look after the turkeys in the poultry-yard.

But little fool Ivan he set beside himself, and made him the chief over the Boyars, and the captain of the captains. And long did they feast together in gladness of heart, till everything was eaten and everything was drunk up. And little fool Ivan began to rule the realm, and his rule was wise and terrible, and on the death of his father-in-law he took his place. His children were many, and his subjects loved him, and his neighbours feared him, but the Tsarina Baktriana was just as beautiful in her old age as when she was young.

THE LITTLE FEATHER OF FENIST THE BRIGHT FALCON.

Once upon a time there was an old widower who lived with his three daughters. The elder and the middle one were fond of show and finery, but the youngest only troubled herself about household affairs although she was of a loveliness which no pen can describe and no tale can tell. One day the old man got ready to go to market in the town, and said: " Now, my dear daughters, say ! what shall I buy for you at the fair ? "—The eldest daughter said : " Buy me, dear dad, a new dress ! "—The middle daughter said : " Buy me, dear dad, a silk kerchief ! "—But the youngest daughter said : " Buy me, dear dad, a little scarlet flower ! "—The old man went to the fair ; he bought for his eldest daughter a new dress, for his middle daughter a silk kerchief, but though he searched the whole town through he could not find a little scarlet flower. He was already on his way back

when there met him a little old man, whom he knew
not, and this little old man was carrying a little
scarlet flower. Our old man was delighted, and he
asked the stranger: "Sell me thy little scarlet flower,
thou dear little old man!"—The old man answered
him: "My little scarlet flower is not for sale, 'tis
mine by will, it has no price and cannot be priced,
but I'll let thee have it as a gift if thou wilt marry
thy youngest daughter to my son!"—"And who then
is thy son, dear old man?"—"My son is the good and
valiant warrior-youth Fenist the bright falcon. By
day he dwells in the sky beneath the high clouds, at
night he descends to the earth as a lovely youth."—
Our old man fell a-thinking; if he did not take the
little scarlet flower he would grieve his daughter, and
if he did take it there was no knowing what sort of
a match he would be making. He thought and
thought, and at last he took the little scarlet flower, for
it occurred to him that if this Fenist the bright falcon,
who was thus to be wedded to his daughter, did not
please him, it would be possible to break the match
off. But no sooner had the strange old man given
him the little scarlet flower than he vanished from
before his eyes just as if he had never met him at all.
The old man scratched his head and began to ponder
still more earnestly: "I don't like the look of it at
all!" he said, and when he got home he gave his elder

daughters their things, and his youngest daughter her little scarlet flower, and said to her: "I don't like thy little scarlet flower a bit, my daughter; I don't like it at all!"—"Wherefore so vexed at it, dear father?" quoth she. Then he stooped down and whispered in her ear: "The little scarlet flower of thine is willed away; it has no price, and money could not buy it me—I have married thee beforehand for it to the son of the strange old man whom I met in the way, to Fenist the bright falcon." And he told her everything that the old man had told him of his son. "Grieve not, dear father!" said the daughter; "judge not of my intended by the sight of thine eyes, for though he come a-flying, we shall love him all the same." And the lovely daughter shut herself up in her little gabled chamber, put her little scarlet flower in water, opened her window, and looked forth into the blue distance. Scarcely had the sun settled down behind the forest when, whence he came who knows, Fenist the bright falcon darted up in front of her little window. He had feathers like flowers, he lit upon the balustrade, fluttered into the little window, flopped down upon the floor, and turned into a goodly young warrior. The damsel was terrified, she very nearly screamed; but the good youth took her tenderly by the hand, looked tenderly into her eyes, and said: "Fear me not, my destined bride! Every evening until our marriage I will come flying to thee; whenever thou placest in the window the little scarlet flower I'll appear before thee. And here is a little feather out of my little wing, and whatever thou mayest desire, go but out on the balcony and wave this little feather—and immediately it will appear before thee." Then Fenist the bright falcon kissed his bride and fluttered out of the window again. And he found great favour in her eyes, and from henceforth she placed the little scarlet flower in the window every evening, and so it was that whenever she placed it there the goodly warrior-youth, Fenist the bright falcon, came down to her.

Thus a whole week passed by, and Sunday came round. The elder sisters decked themselves out to go to church, and attired themselves in their new things, and began to laugh at their younger sister. "What art thou going to wear?" said they; "thou hast no new things at all." And she answered: "No, I have nothing, so I'll stay at home." But she bided her time, went out on the balcony, waved her flowery feather in the right direction, and, whence I know not, there appeared before her a crystal carriage and stud-horses and servants in gold galloon, and they brought for her a splendid dress embroidered with precious stones. The lovely damsel sat in the carriage, and went to church. When she entered the church,

every one looked at her, and marvelled at her beauty
and her priceless splendour. "Some Tsarevna or
other has come to our church, depend upon it!"
the good people whispered among themselves. When
the service was over, our beauty got into her carriage
and rolled home; got into the balcony, waved her
flowery feather over her left shoulder, and in an
instant the carriage and the servants and the rich
garments had disappeared. The sisters came home
and saw her sitting beneath the little window as
before: "Oh, sister!" cried they, "thou hast no idea
what a lovely lady was at mass this morning; 'twas a
thing marvellous to behold, but not to be described
by pen or told in tales."

Two more weeks passed by, and two more Sundays,
and the lovely damsel threw dust in the eyes of the
people as before, and took in her sisters, her father,
and all the other orthodox people. But on the last
occasion, when she was taking off her finery, she forgot to take out of her hair her diamond pin. The
elder sisters came from church, and began to tell her
about the lovely Tsarevna, and as their eyes fell upon
her hair they cried with one voice: "Ah! little sister,
what is that thou hast got?" The lovely damsel
cried also, and ran off into her little room beneath
the gables. And from that time forth the sisters
began to watch the damsel, and to listen of a night at

her little room, and discovered and perceived how at dawn Fenist the bright falcon fluttered out of her little window and disappeared behind the dark woods. And the sisters thought evil of their younger sister. And they strewed pieces of broken glass on the window-sill of their sister's little dormer chamber, and stuck sharp knives and needles there, that Fenist the bright falcon when he lit down upon the window might wound himself on the knives. And at night Fenist the bright falcon flew down and beat vainly with his wings, and beat again, but could not get through the little window, but only wounded himself on the knives and cut and tore his wings. And the bright falcon lamented and fluttered upwards, and cried to the fair damsel: "Farewell, lovely damsel! farewell, my betrothed! Thou shalt see me no more in thy little dormer chamber! Seek me in the land of Thrice-nine, in the empire of Thrice-ten. The way thither is far, thou must wear out slippers of iron, thou must break to pieces a staff of cast-iron, thou must fret away reins of stone, before thou canst find me, good maiden!" And at the self-same hour a heavy sleep fell upon the damsel, and through her sleep she heard these words yet could not awaken. In the morning she awoke, and lo! knives and needles were planted on the window-sill, and blood was trickling from them. All pale and distraught, she wrung her hands and cried: "Lo! my distresses have destroyed my darling beloved!" And the same hour she packed up and started from the house and went to seek her bright-white love, Fenist the shining falcon.

The damsel went on and on through many gloomy forests, she went through many dreary morasses, she went through many barren wildernesses, and at last she came to a certain wretched little hut. She tapped at the window and cried: "Host and hostess, shelter me, a poor damsel, from the dark night!" An old woman came out upon the threshold: "We crave thy pardon, lovely damsel! Whither art thou going, lovey-dovey?"—"Alas! granny, I seek my beloved Fenist the bright falcon. Wilt thou not tell me where to find him?"—"Nay, I know not, but pray go to my middle sister, she will show thee the right way; and lest thou shouldst stray from the path, take this little ball; whithersoever it rolls, thither will be thy way!" The lovely damsel passed the night with the old woman, and on the morrow, when she was departing, the old woman gave her a little gift. "Here," said she, "is a silver spinning-board and a golden spindle; thou wilt spin a spindle full of flax and draw out threads of gold. The time will come when my gift will be of service to thee." The damsel thanked her, and followed the rolling ball. Whether 'twere a long time or a short matters not, but the ball rolled all the way to another little hut. The damsel opened the door and the second old woman opened it. The old woman asked her questions and said to her: "Thou hast still a long way to go, damsel, and it will be no light matter to find thy betrothed. But look now! when thou comest to my elder sister she will be able to tell thee better than I can. But take this gift from me for thy journey—a silver saucer and a golden apple. The time will come when they will be of use to thee." The damsel passed the night in the hut, and then went on further after the rolling ball; she went through the woods further and further, and at every step the woods grew blacker and denser, and the tops of the trees reached to the very sky. The ball rolled right up to the last hut; an old woman came out upon the threshold and invited the lovely damsel to take shelter from the dark night. The damsel told the old woman whither she was going and what she sought. "Thine is a bad business, my child!" said the old woman; "thy Fenist the bright falcon is betrothed to the Tsarevna over-sea, and will shortly be married to her. When thou gettest out of the wood on to the shores of the blue sea, sit on a little stone, take out thy silver spinning-board and thy golden spindle and sit down and spin, and the bride of Fenist the bright falcon will come out to thee and will buy thy spindle from thee, but thou must take no money for it, only ask to see the flowery feathers of Fenist the bright falcon!" The damsel went on further, and the road grew lighter and lighter, and behold! there was the blue sea; free and boundless it lay before her, and there, far, far away above the surface of the sea, bright as a burning fire, gleamed the golden summits of the marble palace halls. "Surely that is the realm of my betrothed which is visible from afar!" thought the lovely damsel, and she sat upon the little stone, took out her silver spinning-board and her golden spindle, and began spinning flax and drawing golden thread out of it. And all at once, she saw coming to her along the sea-shore, a certain Tsarevna, with her nurses and her guards and her faithful servants, and she came up to her and watched her working, and began to bargain with her for her silver spinning-board and her golden spindle. "I will give them to thee for nothing, Tsarevna, only let me look on Fenist the bright falcon!" For a long time the Tsarevna would not consent, but at last she said: "Very well, come and look at him when he is lying down to rest after dinner, and drive the flies away from him!" And she took from the damsel the silver spinning-board and the golden spindle and went to her terem, made Fenist the bright falcon drunk after dinner with a drink of magic venom, and then admitted the damsel when an unwakable slumber had overpowered him. The damsel sat behind his pillow, and her tears flowed over him in streams. "Awake, arise, Fenist the bright falcon!" said she to her love; "I, thy lovely damsel, have come to thee from afar; I have worn out slippers of iron, I have ground down a staff of steel, I have fretted away reins of stone; everywhere and all times have I been seeking thee, my love." But Fenist the bright falcon slept on, nor knew nor felt that the lovely damsel was weeping and mourning over him. Then the Tsarevna also came in, and bade them lead out the lovely damsel, and awoke Fenist the bright falcon. "I have slept for long," said he to his bride, "and yet it seemed to me as if some one has been here and wept and lamented over me."—"Surely thou hast dreamt it in thy dreams?" said the Tsarevna; "I myself was sitting here all the time, and suffered not the flies to light on thee."

The next day the damsel again sat by the sea, and held in her hands the silver saucer and rolled the little golden apple about on it. The Tsarevna came out walking again, went up to her, looked on and said, "Sell me thy toy!"—"My toy is not merchandise, but an inheritance; let me but look once more on Fenist the bright falcon, and thou shalt have it as a gift."—"Very well, come again in the evening, and drive the flies away from my bridegroom!" And again she gave Fenist the bright falcon a drink of magic sleeping venom and admitted the lovely damsel to his pillow. And the lovely damsel began to weep over her love, and at last one of the burning tears fell from her eyes upon his cheeks. Then Fenist the bright falcon awoke from his heavy slumbers and cried, "Alas! who was it who burned me?"—"Oh, darling of my desires!" said the lovely damsel, "I, thy maiden, have come to thee from afar. I have worn out shoes of iron, I have worn down staves of steel, I have gnawed away wafers of stone, and have sought thee everywhere, my beloved! This is the second day that I, thy damsel, have sorrowed over thee, and thou wokest not from thy slumber, nor made answer to my words!" Then only did Fenist the bright falcon know his beloved again, and was so overjoyed that words cannot tell of it. And the damsel told him all that had happened, how her wicked sisters had envied her, how she had wandered from land to land, and how the Tsarevna had bartered him for toys. Fenist fell in love with her more than ever, kissed her on her sugary mouth, and bade them set the bells a-ringing without delay, and assemble the Boyars and the Princes and the men of every degree in the market-place. And he began to ask them, "Tell me, good people, and answer me

The Damsel went on further, and the road grew lighter and lighter, and behold! there was the blue sea

The Damsel went on further, and the road grew lighter and lighter, and behold! there was the blue sea

according to good sense, which bride ought I to take to wife and shorten the sorrow of life: her who sold me, or her who bought me back again?" And the people declared with one voice, "Her who bought thee back again!" And Fenist the bright falcon did so. They crowned him at the altar the same day in wedlock with the lovely damsel. The wedding was joyous and boisterous and magnificent. I also was at this wedding, and drank wine and mead, and the bumpers overflowed, and every one had his fill, and the beard was wet when the mouth was dry.

THE TALE OF THE PEASANT DEMYAN.

WHETHER it is a long time ago or a short time ago I cannot say, but I know that once upon a time, in a certain village, dwelt a peasant who was headstrong and hot-tempered, and his name was Demyan. He was austere and hard and stern, always seeking an occasion to quarrel, and dealing hardly with whomsoever he fell out. Whatever any one said or did to him, he was always ready with his fists. He would invite a neighbour to be his guest, for instance, and force him to eat, and if the neighbour hung back a bit for bashfulness or courtesy, our peasant would pitch into him at once and cry, "In a strange house obey thy host!"

Now this is what happened one day. A smart, sturdy young fellow came to little Demyan as a guest, and our peasant regaled him finely, and filled the table with meat and drink. The young fellow pulled everything towards himself, dish after dish, and munched away in silence with both cheeks crammed full. Our peasant stared and stared, and at last he took off his cloak and said, "Take off thy blouse, and put on my cloak!" But he thought to himself, "He is sure to refuse, and then I'll show him something!" But the youth put on the cloak, tied it round with his girdle, bowed low and said, "Well, little father! I thank thee for thy gift. I dare not refuse, for in a strange house one must obey the host."

The host was furious; he wanted to pick a quarrel with him now at any price, so he ran into the stable, got out his best horse, and said to the youth, "Nothing is too good for thee! Here, mount my horse, and take it away as thine own!" But he thought, "He'll be sure to refuse, and then I'll teach him a lesson." But the youth again said, "In a strange house we must always obey the host!" Only when he was fairly mounted did he turn round to the peasant Demyan and cry, "Farewell, mine host! Nobody pushed thee, but thou didst fall into the ditch of thine own self!" and he trotted out of the courtyard right away.

But the host looked after him, shook his head, and said, "The scythe has struck upon a stone!"[1]

[1] *I.e.* I've met my match at last.

THE ENCHANTED RING.

In a certain kingdom in a certain empire, there lived, once upon a time, an old man and an old woman, and they had a son called little Martin. Time went on, the old man fell ill and died, and though he had worked hard all his days, the only inheritance he left behind him was two hundred rubles.[1] The old woman did not want to waste this money, but what was to be done? There was nothing to eat, so she had to have recourse to the pot containing the patrimony. The old woman counted out a hundred rubles, and sent her son to town to buy provision of bread for a whole year. So Martin the widow's son went to town. He went past the meat market, and saw crowds of people gathered together, and his ears were deafened by the din and noise and racket. Little Martin went into the midst of the throng and saw that the butchers had caught a

[1] Twenty pounds.

terrier, and had fastened it to a post, and were beating it unmercifully. Little Martin was sorry for the poor dog, and said to the butchers, "My brothers! why do you beat the poor dog so unmercifully?"—"Why should we not beat him, when he has spoiled a whole quarter of beef?"—"Yet, beat him not, my brothers! 'Twere better to sell him to me!"—"Buy him if you like then!" said the butchers, mockingly, "but for such a treasure as that we could not take less than a hundred rubles."—"Well, one hundred rubles is only one hundred rubles after all!" replied little Martin, and he drew out the money and gave it for the dog. But the dog's name was Jurka.[1] Martin then went home, and his mother asked him, "What hast thou bought?"—"Why look, I have bought Jurka!" replied her son. His mother fell a-scolding him, and reproached him bitterly: "Art thou not ashamed? Soon we shall not have a morsel to eat, and thou hast gone and thrown away so much money on a pagan dog." The next day the old woman sent her son into the town again, and said to him, "Now there is our last one hundred rubles, buy with it provision of bread. To-day I will collect together the scrapings of the meal-tub and bake us fritters, but to-morrow there will not even be that!" Little Martin got to town and walked along the

[1] Growlér.

streets and looked about him, and he saw a boy who had fastened a cord round a cat's neck and was dragging it off to drown it. "Stop!" shrieked Martin, "whither art thou dragging Vaska?"[1]—"I am dragging him off to be drowned!"—"Why, what has he done?"—"He is a great rascal. He has stolen a whole goose."—"Don't drown him, far better sell him to me!"—"I'll take nothing less than one hundred rubles!"—"Well, one hundred rubles is only one hundred rubles after all; here! take the money!" And he took Vaska from the boy. "What hast thou bought, my son?" asked his mother when he got home.—"Why the cat Vaska!"—"And what besides?"—"Well, perhaps there's some money still left, and then we can buy something else."—"Oh, oh, oh! what a fool thou art!" screeched the old woman. "Go out of the house this instant and beg thy bread from the stranger!"

Martin dared not gainsay his mother, so he took Jurka and Vaska with him and went into the neighbouring village to seek work. And there met him a rich farmer. "Whither art thou going?" said he. "I want to hire myself out as a day-labourer."—"Come to me then. I take labourers without any contract, but if thou serve me well for a year thou shalt not lose by it." Martin agreed, and for a whole

[1] Pussy.

THE ENCHANTED RING.

year he worked for this farmer without ceasing. The time of payment came round. The farmer led Martin into the barn, showed him two full sacks, and said, "Take which thou wilt." Martin looked; in one of the sacks was riches, in the other sand, and he thought to himself, "That's not done without a reason; there's some trickery here. I'll take the sand; something will come of it no doubt." So Martin put the sack of sand on his back, and went to seek another place. He went on and on, and strayed into a dark and dreary wood. In the midst of the wood was a field, and on the field a fire was burning, and in the fire a maiden was sitting; and it was such a lovely maiden that it was a delight to look at her. And the Beauty said to him, "Martin the widow's son, if thou wishest to find happiness, save me. Extinguish this flame with the sand which thou hast gotten for thy faithful service."—"Well, really," thought Martin, "why should I go on dragging this load about on my shoulders? Far better to help a body with it." So he undid his sack and emptied all the sand on the fire. The fire immediately went out, but the lovely damsel turned into a serpent, bounded on to the bosom of the good youth, wound itself round his neck, and said, "Fear me not, Martin the widow's son. Go boldly into the land of Thrice-ten, into the underground realm where my dear father rules.

Only mark this; he will offer thee lots of gold and silver and precious stones; thou, however, must take none of them, but beg him for the little ring off his little finger. That ring is no common ring; if thou move it from one hand to the other twelve young heroes will immediately appear, and whatever thou dost bid them do they will do it in a single night."

Then the young man set out on his long, long journey, whether 'twere a long time or a short I know not, but at last he drew nigh to the kingdom of Thrice-ten, and came to a place where a huge stone lay across the way. Here the snake leaped from his neck, lit on the damp ground, and turned into the former lovely damsel. "Follow me," said she to Martin, and showed him a little hole beneath the stone. For a long time they went through this underground way, and came into a wide plain beneath the open sky; and in this plain a castle was built entirely of porphyry, with a roof of golden fish-scales, with sharp-pointed golden pinnacles. "That's where my father lives, the Tsar of this underground region," said the lovely damsel to Martin.

The wanderers entered the castle, and the Tsar met them kindly and made them welcome. "My dear daughter," said he to the lovely damsel, "I did not expect to see thee here. Where hast thou been knocking about all these years?"—"Dear father, and light of my eyes, I should have been lost altogether but for this good youth, who saved me from an unavoidable death!" The Tsar turned, looked with a friendly eye at Martin, and said to him, " I thank thee, good youth. I am ready to reward thee for thy good deeds with whatever thou desirest. Take of my gold and silver and precious stones as much as thy soul longs for."—" I thank thee, Sovereign Tsar, for thy good words. But I want no precious stones, nor silver, nor gold; but if thou of thy royal grace and favour would indeed reward me, then give me, I pray, the ring from the little finger of thy royal hand. Whenever I look upon that ring I'll think of thee; but if ever I meet with a bride after mine own heart I will give it to her." The Tsar immediately took off the ring, gave it to Martin, and said, " By all means, good youth, take the ring, and may it be to thy health! But mark this one thing: tell no one that this ring of thine is no common ring, or it will be to thy hurt and harm!"

Martin the widow's son thanked the Tsar and took the ring, and returned by the same way through which he had reached the underground realm. He returned to his native place, sought out his old widowed mother, and lived and dwelt with her without either want or care. Yet for all the good life he led, Martin seemed sorrowful; and why should he not? for Martin wanted to marry, and the bride of his choice was not his like in birth, for she was a king's daughter. So he consulted his mother, and sent her away as his matchmaker, and said to her, "Go to the King himself, and woo for me the thrice-lovely Princess."—"Alas! my dear son," said his old mother, "'twould be far better for thee if thou wert to chop thine own wood.[1] But what art thou thinking of? How can I go to the King and ask him for his daughter for thee? 'Twould be as much as thy head and my head were worth."—"Fear not, dear mother! If I send thee, thou mayest go boldly. And mind thou dost not come back from the King without an answer."

So the old woman dragged herself to the royal palace. She went into the royal courtyard, and without being announced she went right up to the very staircase of the King. The guards shook their arms at her as a sign that nobody was allowed to go there, but she didn't trouble her head about that one bit, but kept on creeping up. Then all the royal lacqueys came running up, and took the old woman under the arms and would have quite gently led her down again; but the old woman made such a to-do and fell a-shrieking so loudly that it pierced through everything, and the King himself in his lofty carved

[1] *I. e.* go about thine own errand.

palace heard the noise, and looked out of his little window into the courtyard, and saw his servants dragging an old woman down the staircase, and preventing her from entering the royal apartments, while the old woman was resisting and shrieking with all her might. "I won't go out! I have come to the King on a good errand!" The King commanded them to admit the old woman. The old woman entered the carved palace, and saw sitting in the front corner, on the high carved throne, on cushions of purple velvet, the King in state, holding a council in the midst of his grandees and his councillors. The old woman invoked the aid of the holy ikons,[1] and bowed very low before the King. "What hast thou to say, old woman?" asked the King.—"Now, lo! I I have come to your Majesty—be not wroth at my words—I have come to your Majesty as a matchmaker!"—"Art thou in thy senses, old woman?" cried the King, and his brow was wrinkled with a frown.—"Nay, O father-king! pray do not be angry; pray give me an answer. You have the wares—a little daughter, a beauty; I have the purchaser—a young man, so wise, so cunning, a master of every trade, so that you could not find a better son-in-law. Tell me, therefore, straight out, won't you give your daughter to my son?" The King

[1] Pictures of the Saints.

listened and listened to the old woman, and at first his frown was blacker than night, but he thought to himself, "Does it become me, a king, to be wroth with a silly old woman?" And the royal councillors were amazed, for they saw the wrinkles on the King's forehead smoothing out, and the King looked at the old woman with a smile. "If thy son is so cunning, and a master of every trade, let him build me within twenty-four hours a palace more gorgeous than my own, and let him hang a crystal bridge between this palace and my palace, and let luxuriant apple trees grow up all along this bridge, and let them bear silver and golden pippins, and let birds of paradise sing within these apple trees. And on the right-hand side of this crystal bridge let him build a cathedral five storeys high, with golden pinnacles, where he may receive the wedding crown with my daughter, and where the marriage may be celebrated. But if thy son fulfil not all this, then for thy and his presumption I will have you both smeared with tar and rolled in feathers and down, and hanged up in cages in the market-place as a laughing-stock to all good people." And the King condescended to smile still more pleasantly, and his grandees and his councillors held their sides, and rolled about the floor for laughter, and they began with one voice to praise his wisdom and thought amongst themselves.

"What fun it will be to see the old woman and her son hung up in cages! 'Tis as plain as daylight; a beard will sooner grow out of the palm of his hand than he be able to accomplish so shrewd a task." The poor old woman was near to swooning. "What!" said she to the King, "is this thy final sovereign word? Is this what I must say to my son?"—"Yes, thus must thou say: if he accomplish this task, I will give him my daughter; if he does not accomplish it, I will put you both into cages."

The poor old woman went home more alive than dead. She staggered from side to side, and shed floods of scalding tears. When she saw Martin, she began screeching at him from afar. "Did not I tell thee, my son, to go and chop thine own wood? Now thou seest that our poor little heads are lost." And she told her son all about it. "Cheer up, mother," said little Martin, "pray to God and lie down to sleep, the morning is always wiser than the evening." But he himself went out of the hut, took his little ring from one hand and put it on the other, and the twelve youths immediately appeared before him and said, "What dost thou require?" He told them of the royal task, and the twelve youths answered, "To-morrow, everything will be ready."

The King awoke next morning, and lo! right in front of his palace towered another palace, and a crystal bridge led from one to the other. Along the sides of the bridge stood luxuriant apple trees, and upon them hung golden pippins, and birds of paradise were singing in the trees; and on the right hand of the bridge, blazing like fire in the sun, stood the cathedral with its golden pinnacles; and the bells of the cathedral were ringing and pealing in all directions. The King had to keep his word. He raised his son-in-law high in rank, gave him a rich inheritance with his daughter, and he took her to wife. Great was the wedding-feast. The wine flowed in streams, and they drank of mead and beer till they could drink no more.

So Martin lived in his palace, and he ate of the best and drank of the best, and his life went as smoothly as cheese with butter. But the Princess did not love him at heart, and when she reflected that they had not married her to the son of a tsar, or the son of a king, or even to a prince from across the sea, but to simple Martin the widow's son, her wrath waxed hot within her. And she fell a-thinking by what means she might best rid herself of a husband she hated. So she took care to caress him, and flatter him, and waited upon him herself, and made him comfortable, and when they were quite alone she would ask him what it was that made him so wise and clever. And it happened one day that when he had been the King's guest, and had drunk and made merry with all his lords one after another, and had returned home and laid him down to rest, that the Princess came to him and caressed him, and coaxed him with wheedling words, and made him drunk with strong mead, and in that way found out what she wanted to know, for Martin told her all about his enchanted ring, and showed her how to turn it. And no sooner was little Martin asleep and snoring, than the Princess took off the enchanted ring from his little finger, went forth into the broad courtyard, moved the ring from one finger to the other, and the twelve youths immediately appeared before her. "What is thy pleasure, and what is thy desire?"—"That to-morrow morning there may be neither palace, nor bridge, nor cathedral on this spot, but only a wretched little hut as heretofore, and cast this drunkard into it, but remove me far from him into the Empire of Thrice-ten."—"It shall be done," replied the twelve youths with one voice.

In the morning, when the King awoke, he felt inclined to go and pay a visit to his son-in-law and his daughter, so he went out upon the balcony, and lo! there was neither palace, nor bridge, nor cathedral, nor garden. In place of them stood a wretched old hut, leaning on one side, and scarce able to stand at all. The King sent for his son-in-law, and began asking him what it all meant; but little Martin could only stare blankly at him without uttering a word. And the King bade them sit in judgment on his son-in-law for deceiving him by magic, and destroying his daughter, the thrice-lovely Princess, and they condemned Martin to be put on the top of a lofty stone column with nothing to eat or drink; there he was to be left to die of hunger.

Then it was that Jurka and Vaska remembered how little Martin had saved them from an evil death, and they came and laid their heads together about it. Jurka growled and snarled, and was ready to tear every one to bits, for his master's sake; but Vaska purred and hummed and scratched himself behind the ear with his velvet paw, and began to think the matter over. And the artful cat hit upon a plan, and said to Jurka, "Let us go for a walk about the town, and as soon as we meet a roll-baker with a tin on his head, you run between his legs and knock the tin off his head, and I'll be close behind and immediately seize the rolls, and take them to master." No sooner said than done. Jurka and the cat took a run into the town, and they met a roll-baker. He was carrying a tin on his head, and he looked about him on all sides and cried with a loud voice, "Hot rolls, hot rolls, fresh from the oven!" Jurka ran between his legs, the baker stumbled, the tin fell, and all the rolls were scattered about. But while the angry baker was chasing Jurka, Vaska hid all the rolls in the hedges. Then the cat and Jurka ran to the tower where Martin was placed, dragged with them the stores of bread, and Vaska scrambled up to the top, looked in at the little window, called to his master, and said, "Alive, eh?"—"Scarcely alive!" replied little Martin; "I am quite exhausted from want of food, and it will not be long before I die of hunger."—"Don't grieve; wait a bit, and we'll feed you," said Vaska, and he began to drag the food up from below—rolls and cakes, and all kinds of bread, till he had dragged up for his master a large store. Then he said, "Master, Jurka and I will go to the kingdom of Thrice-ten, and get you back your enchanted ring. Take care to make the bread last till we return." Then they both took leave of their master, and departed on their long journey.

They ran on and on, and they smelt out the scent everywhere and followed it; paid great attention to what people told them; carefully made friends with all the other dogs and cats they met; asked about the Princess, and found out at last that they were not far from the kingdom of Thrice-ten, whither she had told the twelve youths to carry her. They ran into the kingdom, went to the palace, and made friends with all the dogs and cats there, asked them all about the Princess's ways, and turned the conversation to the subject of the enchanted ring; but no one could give them certain information about it. But one day it happened that Vaska went a-hunting in the royal cellars. There he waylaid a big fat mouse, threw himself upon it, dug his cruel claws into it, and was going to begin with its head, when the big mouse spoke to him: "Dear little Vaska, don't hurt me, don't kill me. Perhaps I may be of service to you. I'll do all I can for you. But if you kill me, the Mouse-Tsar, all my mousey tsardom will fall to pieces."—"Very well," said Vaska; "I'll spare you; but this is the service you must do me. In this palace dwells the Princess, the wicked wife of our master; she has stolen from him his wonder-working ring; till you have got me that ring, I will not let you out of my claws under any pretence whatever."—"Agreed," said the Mouse-Tsar, "I'll try"; and he piped and whistled all his people together. A countless multitude of mice assembled, both small and great, and they sat all round the cat Vaska, and waited to hear what the Mouse-Tsar would say to them from beneath Vaska's claws. And the Mouse-Tsar said to them: "Whichever of you shall get the wonder-working ring from the Princess, he will save me from a cruel death, and I will raise him to the highest place about my person." Then a little mouse rose up and said: "I have often been in the Princess's bed-chamber, and I've noticed that the Princess's eye rests more often on a certain little ring than on anything else. In the daytime she wears it on her little finger, but at night she stuffs it into her mouth behind her cheeks. If you wait a bit, I'll get you that ring." And the little mouse ran into the Princess's bed-chamber and waited till night, and as soon as ever the Princess was asleep, it wriggled into her bed, picked the down out of her swan-feathered bolster, and strewed it all about under her nose. The fine down went up the Princess's nose and into her mouth, she sprang up and began to sneeze and cough, and spat out the enchanted ring on to the counterpane. The little mouse immediately snatched it up, and ran off with it to save the life of the Mouse-Tsar.

Vaska and Jurka set off to bring their master the wonder-working ring. Whether they took a long time or a short time matters not, but they arrived at last, and ran to the tower in which Martin was put to die from starvation. The cat immediately climbed up to the window, and called to its master, "Art thou alive, Martin the widow's son?"—"I am scarce able to keep body and soul together. This is the third day I have been sitting here without bread."—"Well, thy woes are over now. There will be a feast in *your* street now [1]; we have brought you your ring." Martin was overjoyed, and began to stroke the cat, and the cat rubbed itself against him, and began purring its own little songs through its nose; but at the bottom of the tower Jurka was leaping and whining and barking for joy, and leaping high in the air. Martin took the ring and turned it from one hand to the other. The twelve youths immediately appeared: "What is thy pleasure, and what thy command?"—"Give me to eat and drink till I can eat and drink no more, and let cunning music be played on the top of this tower to me all day." When the music began to play, the good folks hastened to the King, and told him that little Martin was up to no good in the tower there. "He ought to have ceased to be among the living long ago," they said, "and yet he is having such a merry time of it on the top of the tower. They are stamping with their feet, and knocking their plates, and clashing their glasses, and such splendid music is playing, that you can't help listening to it." The King sent an express messenger to the tower, and there he stood and listened to the music; the King sent his highest officer, and there they all remained standing, and opened wide their ears. The King himself went to the tower, and the music seemed to turn him into a

---

[1] *I. e.* It will be your turn to triumph now.

statue. But little Martin again called his twelve youths, and said to them, "Restore my old palace, as it was before; throw a crystal bridge across from it to the royal palace; let the former five-storeyed cathedral stand by the side of the palace; and let my faithless wife also be found in the palace." And while he was yet expressing the wish, the whole thing was done. And he went out of the tower, took his father-in-law the King by the hand, led him into the palace, led him up to the sleeping-chamber, where the Princess, in fear and trembling, awaited an evil death, and said to the King, "My dear little father-in-law, a great deal of trouble and anguish has befallen me from living with thy daughter; what shall we sentence her to?"—"My dear son-in-law, let mercy prevail over justice; exhort her with good words, and live with her as heretofore." And Martin listened to his father-in-law, upbraided his wife for her treachery, and to the end of his life he never parted with the ring, nor with Jurka and Vaska, and saw no more misery.

THE BRAVE LABOURER.

A YOUNG fellow entered the service of a miller. The miller sent him to throw grain on the scoop, but the labourer, not knowing how to set about it, went and strewed the wheat on the mill-stone. The mill-wheel went round, and all the grain was scattered about. The master miller, when he came to the mill, and saw the scattered grain, sent the workman about his business. The workman went home and thought to himself, "Well, I haven't been very long working at the mill." So he went on his way thinking to himself, and so he missed the way to his own village. He strayed among the bushes, and wandered and wandered about till he came to a stream, and on the stream stood an empty mill, and in this mill he resolved to pass the night.

The dumb midnight hour approached; the labourer could not sleep in the empty mill; he listened to every rustling sound, and suddenly it was as though he heard some one approaching the mill. The poor labourer started up more dead than alive, and hid himself in the scoop. Three men entered the mill. Judging from their appearance they were no good people, but robbers. They lit a fire in the mill, and began to divide amongst themselves a rich booty. And one of the robbers said to the others, " I will lay my portion underneath the mill." The second said, " I'll shove mine underneath the wheel." But the third said, " I'll conceal my goods in the scoop." But our labourer was lying in the scoop, and he thought, " No man can die twice, but every man *must* die once. I wonder now if I can frighten them. Let us try." And he roared at the top of his voice : " Denis, you come down there ; and you, Phocas, look on that side ; and you, little one, look there, and I'll be here. Stop them, don't let them go, and beat them without mercy." The robbers were terrified, threw down their booty, took to their heels straightway, and the labourer took their booty and returned home richer than rich.

THE SAGE DAMSEL.

An old man and an old woman died, and left behind them a son young in years, who was rich neither in wits nor goods. His uncle took him home, gave him to eat and drink, and when he grew up sent him to watch the sheep. And one day he sent for his kinsman and resolved to test his wits; so he said to him: "Here thou hast a flock of sheep, drive them to market and make profit out of them in such a way that both thou and the sheep shall get fat upon it, and the sheep be all brought back whole, and yet all, to the very last one, be sold for ready money."

"How is that to be managed?" thought the orphan, who drove the sheep into the open field, sat by the roadside, and fell a-thinking. A lovely damsel passed by that way, and she said to him: "Of what art thou thinking, good youth?"

"Why should I not be thinking? My grandfather has taken a spite at last against me, a poor orphan; he has given me a task to do, and cudgel my brains as I may I cannot see how it is to be done."

"What task has he given thee?"

"Well, look here; he says, 'Go to market, drive those sheep thither and make a profit out of them, but so that thou and the sheep shall grow fat upon it, and the sheep be brought back whole, all down to the last one, and yet be sold for ready money.'"

"Well, that's no very tricky task," replied the damsel. "Shear the sheep, take the fleeces to market and sell them, then thou wilt make a profit out of them, and the sheep will remain whole, and thou wilt be able to feed thyself on the profits."

The youth thanked the damsel and did as she said. He sheared the sheep, sold their fleeces at the market, drove home the flock, and gave the money he had made out of them to his uncle. "Good," said the uncle to the nephew; "but I am sure thou didst not work this out with thine own wits, eh? Didn't some one or other teach it thee?" The youth confessed: "Well, I certainly did not do it by my own wits, but a lovely damsel came by and taught me."—"Well, then, thou must take this sage young damsel to wife. 'Twill be a very good thing for thee, for here art thou an orphan with neither stick nor stone of thy own, and nothing much in the way of wits either!"—"I don't mind if I do marry her," said the nephew to his uncle.—"All right, but thou must render me this one service. Take corn to town to the bazaar. According as thou dost sell it and return again, I'll wed thee to this damsel."

So the nephew went to town to sell the uncle's corn, and on the way he met a rich miller.—"Why art thou off to town?" said the miller.—"I am going to the bazaar to sell my uncle's corn."—"Then we'll go to town together."—So they went along the road together, the miller in his gig with his plump brown horse, and the orphan in his little cart with his thin gray mare. They encamped side by side in the open field to pass the night there, took out the horses, and themselves lay down to sleep. And it happened that self-same night the gray mare dropped a foal. The rich miller woke earlier than the orphan, saw the foal, and drove him beneath his gig. When the orphan awoke a hot dispute arose between them. The orphan said: "It is my foal, because my mare dropped it." The covetous miller said: "No, 'tis mine, because thy mare dropped it beneath my gig." They wrangled and wrangled till they resolved to go to law about it, and when they arrived in town they went to the court to fight the matter out there. And the judge said to them: "In our town we have introduced this custom into the tribunals, that whoever wants to go to law must first of all guess four riddles. So tell me now: what is the strongest and swiftest thing in the world; what is the fattest thing in the world; and what is the softest, and what the sweetest of all?"

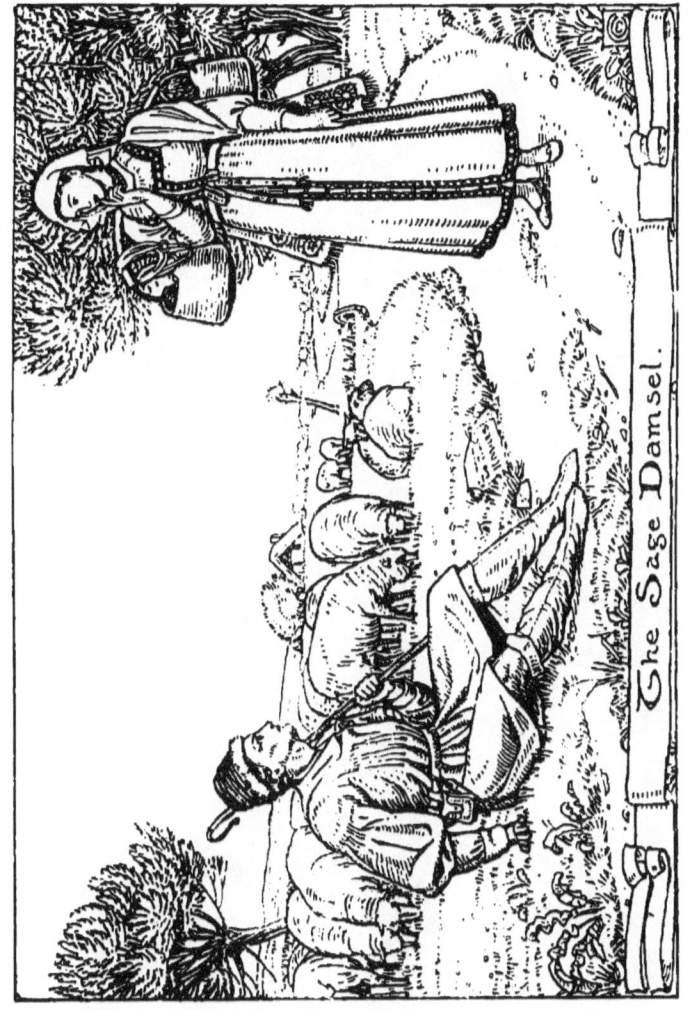

The Sage Damsel.

The Sage Damsel.

The judge gave them three days to guess, and said: "If you guess my riddles, I will judge betwixt you according to law; but if not, don't be angry if I drive you away."

The rich miller went to his wife and told her how the matter stood, and what riddles the judge had given him to guess. "All thy riddles are but simple ones," replied the miller's wife; "if they ask thee what is the strongest and swiftest thing in the world, tell them that my father has a dark-brown horse so strong and nimble that it can run down a hare. And if they ask thee what is the fattest thing in the world, dost thou not know that in our stall we are fattening up a two-year-old boar, and he's getting so fat that his very legs won't be able to hold him up? And as for the third riddle, what is the softest thing in the world, why it's quite plain that that's a down pillow; thou canst not imagine anything softer than that. And if they ask thee what is the sweetest thing in the world, say: 'Why, what sweeter thing can a man have than the wife of his bosom?'"

But the orphan went out of the town into the fields and sat by the roadside and racked his brain. He sat and thought of his misery; and along the road, close to him, passed the self-same lovely damsel. "Why art thou so racking thy brains again, good youth?"— "Why, look here, the judge has given me four such riddles to guess that I shall never be able to guess them all my days," and he told the damsel all about it. The damsel laughed, and said to him: "Go to the judge and say to him, that the strongest and swiftest thing in the world is the wind; that the fattest of all is the earth, for she feeds everything that lives and grows upon her; the softest of all is the palm of the hand, for however soft a man may lie he always puts his hand beneath his head; and there's nothing sweeter in the whole world than sleep." The poor little orphan bowed to the very girdle to the damsel, and said to her: "I thank thee, thou sagest of maidens, for thou hast snatched me from very ruin."

When the three days had passed, the miller and the orphan appeared in court, and told the court the answers to the riddles. Now the Tsar chanced to be on the bench at that time, and the answers of the orphan so pleased him that he ordered that the cause between them should be given in his favour, and that the miller should be driven with shame from the court. After that the Tsar said to the orphan: "Didst thou hit upon these answers thyself, or did some one else tell thee?"—"To tell the truth, they are not my own; the lovely damsel taught me these answers."—"She has taught thee well too, sage indeed must she be. Go to her and tell her in my name that if she be so wise and sensible she must appear before me to-morrow: neither on foot nor on horseback, neither naked nor clothed, and with a present in her hand that is no gift. If she accomplish this I will reward her as becomes a Tsar, and make her higher than the highest." Again the orphan went out of the town, and again he fell a-fretting, and he said to himself: "Why, I don't even know how and have no idea where to find this lovely damsel; what sort of a task is this that I am bidden to give her?" No sooner had he thought this than the sage and lovely damsel again passed by that way. The orphan told her how his guesses had pleased the Tsar, and how he wanted to see the damsel himself and have proof of her wisdom, and how he had promised to reward her. The damsel thought a bit, and then said to the orphan: "Fetch me a long-bearded billy-goat, and a big net for catching fish, and catch me a pair of sparrows. To-morrow morning we'll meet here, and if I get a reward from the Tsar, I'll share it equally with thee."

The orphan carried out the orders of the damsel, and waited for her next morning at the roadside. The damsel appeared, stripped off her sarafan,[1] and wound herself in the long fishing-net from head to foot; then she sat on the goat, took a sparrow in each hand, and bade the orphan lead the way to town. The young man brought her to the Tsar at court, and she bowed low to the Tsar and said: "Behold, O sovereign Tsar! I come to thee neither on foot nor

[1] A long dress without sleeves.

on horseback, neither naked nor clothed, and I have brought a present in my hand which is no gift."—" Where is it?" asked the Tsar. "Here!" and she gave the Tsar the live sparrows, and he was about to take them from her hands when the sparrows wriggled out and flew away. "Well," said the Tsar, "I see thou canst vie even with me in wit. Stay at my court, and look after my children, and I'll give thee a rich recompense."—"Nay, my sovereign lord and Tsar, I cannot accept thy gracious favour; I have promised this good youth to share my reward with him for his services."—"Look now! thou art witty and wise; but in this matter thy head is turned, and thou dost not judge according to reason. I offer thee a high and honourable place with a great recompense; why then canst thou not share this reward with this youth?"—"But how can I share it then?"—"How, thou sage damsel? Why if this good youth be dear to thee, marry him; for honour and recompense, and labour and sorrow and bright-faced joy are shared by husband and wife half and half."—"Thou too art wise, I see, O sovereign Tsar, and I'll gainsay thee no longer," said the lovely damsel. So she took the orphan for her husband, and though the orphan had no very great mind, his heart was simple and good, and he lived with his sage wife all his life in contentment and happiness.

THE PROPHETIC DREAM.

THERE was once upon a time a merchant, and he had two sons, Dmitry and Ivan. Once the father bade his sons good-night, sent them off to bed, and said to them: "Now, children, whatever you see in your dreams, tell it all to me to-morrow morning, and whichever of you hides his dream from me, no good thing will befall him." In the morning the eldest son came to his father and said: "I dreamed, dear father, that my brother Ivan flew high into the sky on twenty eagles."—"Very good!" said the father; "and what didst thou dream, Vania?"[1]— "Well, such rubbish, father, that it is impossible to tell it."—"What dost thou mean? Speak!"—"No, I'll not!"—"Speak, sir, when I bid thee!"—"No, I won't speak, I won't." The father was very angry with his youngest son, and resolved to punish him for his disobedience, so he sent for his overseers and

[1] The short of Ivan, like Jack from John.

bade them strip Ivan naked and tie him to a post at the crossways as tightly as possible. No sooner said than done. The overseers seized hold of him, dragged him far, far away from home to the crossways, where seven roads crossed, tied him by the hands and feet to the post, and left him alone to his fate. The poor youth fared very badly. The sun scorched him, the gnats and flies sucked his blood, hunger and thirst tortured him. Fortunately for Ivan, a young Tsarevich happened to be going along one of these seven roads; he saw the merchant's son, had compassion on him, and bade his attendants untie him from the post, dressed him in his own clothes, and saved him from a cruel death. The Tsarevich took Ivan to his court, gave him to eat and drink, and asked him who had tied him to the post. "My own father, who was angry with me."—"And wherefore, pray? Surely thy fault was not small?"—"Well, in fact, I would not obey him; I would not tell him what I saw in my dreams."—"And for such a trifle as that he condemned thee to so cruel a punishment! The villain! But surely he has outgrown his wits! But what then didst thou see in thy dream?"—"I saw what I cannot even tell unto thee, O Tsarevich!"— "What! Not tell? Not tell me? me, the Tsarevich? What! I saved thee from a cruel death, and thou wilt not do this trifle for me in return? Speak

immediately, or it will not be well with thee!"—
"Nay, Tsarevich! I stick to my word. I haven't
told my father, and I'll not tell thee."—The Tsarevich boiled over with unspeakable rage, and shrieked
to his servants and attendants, "Hi! my faithful
servants, take this good-for-nothing boor, put heavy
irons on his hands, weld grievous fetters to his legs,
and cast him into my deep dungeon!" The servants
did not think twice about their master's commands;
they seized Ivan the merchant's son, loaded his
hands and feet with fetters, and put him as God's
slave in the stone sack. A little and a long time
passed by, and the Tsarevich thought of marrying
the thrice-wise Helena, the first maiden in the whole
earth for beauty and wisdom, so he made ready and
went into the strange country far away to marry this
thrice-wise Helena. Now it happened that the day
after he had gone, his sister the Tsarevna went
walking in the garden hard by the very same
dungeon in which Ivan the merchant's son had been
put. He saw the Tsarevna through the little grated
window, and cried to her with a lamentable voice:
"Dear mother Tsarevna, thy brother will never be
married without my help."—"Who art thou?"
answered the Tsarevna. Ivan named his name and
added: "I suppose thou hast heard, O Tsarevna, of
the trickeries and the cunning wiles of the thrice-

wise Helena? I have heard not once nor twice that she has expedited many wooers into another world; believe me that thy brother also will not be able to marry her without me!"—"And *thou* art able to help the Tsarevich?"—"Able and willing, but the falcon's wings are bound, and no way for him is found."—The Tsarevna bade them release Ivan from his dungeon, and gave him full liberty to do what was in his mind so long as he only helped the Tsarevich to marry. And then Ivan the merchant's son chose him comrades first of all, one by one, and added youth to youth, and they were all as like to each other as if they had been born brothers. He dressed them in mantles of one kind, sewn in one and the same fashion; he mounted them on horses of one colour, and like each other to a hair, and they all mounted and rode away. Twelve was the number of the young comrades of Ivan the merchant's son. They rode for one day, they rode for another day, and on the third day they entered a gloomy forest, and Ivan said to his comrades: "Stay, my brothers, there is here, on the verge of the precipice, an old tree; a hollow, branchless tree; I must look into its hollow trunk and find my fortune there." So he went to the tree he had described and plunged his hand into the hollow trunk, and drew out of it an invisible cap, hid it in his bosom, and returned to his comrades.

And they came to the realm of the thrice-wise Helena, went straight into the capital, sought out the Tsarevich, and begged him: "Take us into thy service, O Tsarevich; we will serve thee with a single heart." The Tsarevich thought the matter over and said: "How can I help taking such gallant youths into my service? perhaps in a strange land they may be of service to me." And to each of them he assigned his post; he made one his equerry, another his cook, but Ivan he bade never to depart from his side.

The next day the Tsarevich attired himself in festal raiment, and went forth to woo the thrice-wise Helena. She received him courteously, regaled him with all manner of rich meats and drinks, and then she said to the Tsarevich: "I don't at all mind being thy wife, but first of all thou must accomplish these tasks. If thou do them I will be thy faithful wife, but if not, thy haughty head shall wag no more on thy stalwart shoulders."—"Why be afraid before the time? tell me thy tasks, thrice-wise Helena!"— "This then is my first task for thee: I shall have ready by to-morrow what I will not tell thee, and for what purpose I do not know; show thy wit, then, and bring me the fellow of it, of thine own devising." The Tsarevich went home from the court by no means happy; his haughty head hung lower than his stalwart shoulders. And Ivan met him and said: "Halve thy grief with me, O Tsarevich, and it will be better for thee."—"Well, look now," said the Tsarevich, "Helena has set me a task that not a single wise man in the world could do"—and he told Ivan all about it. "Well," said Ivan, "'tis not such a great matter after all! Pray to God and lie down to sleep; the morning is wiser than the evening— to-morrow we'll consider the matter." The Tsarevich lay down to sleep, but Ivan the merchant's son put on his invisible cap, went as swiftly as possible to the palace, ran through all the chambers, and made his way right into the bedchamber of the thrice-wise Helena. And then he heard her giving these orders to her favourite servant: "Take this cloth-of-gold to my shoemaker, and let him make me shoes for my feet as soon as possible." The servant ran with all her might, and behind her ran Ivan. The cobbler set to work; the work seemed to burn his fingers, so quickly did he do it; he beat the stuff with his little hammer and stitched it with his needle; a little shoe was quickly ready, and he put it on the little window-sill. Ivan the merchant's son took the little shoe and hid it in his bosom. The shoemaker was in great consternation: what was the meaning of it? His work had vanished from before his eyes. He searched and searched. He rummaged in every corner, but it was all in vain. "What marvel is this?" thought he; "can the unclean spirit[1] be playing his tricks with me?" There was no help for it. He set to work again with his awl, finished the other slipper, and sent it by the servant-maid to the thrice-wise Helena. But Ivan was after her again, crept like a shadow into the palace in his invisible cap, stood behind the shoulders of the thrice-wise Helena, and saw that she sat behind her little table and began to cover the slipper with gold, embroider it with large pearls, and set it thickly with precious stones. Ivan the merchant's son drew his own slipper out of his bosom and began to do the like with it; whenever she took up a little gem, he chose out just such another; wherever she threaded a pearl, he took another and sewed that on too. The thrice-wise Helena finished her work, looked at the slipper, and couldn't admire it enough. She smiled, and thought to herself: "We will see what the Tsarevich will present himself with to-morrow morning." But Ivan the merchant's son awoke the Tsarevich very early next morning, took the slipper from his bosom, and gave it to him. "Go to thy lady and show her this slipper," said he; "there thou hast her first task!" The Tsarevich washed and dressed himself, hastened to his lady, and found

[1] *I. e.* the devil.

her apartments full of Boyars and Grandees, and her Councillors were all assembled there down to the very last one. There was a noise of melody, there came a crash of lively music, the doors of the inner chambers were thrown open, and out came the thrice-wise Helena, sailing along like a white swan. She bowed on all sides, but particularly to the Tsarevich: then she drew out of her pocket the shoe, set with large pearls and adorned with precious stones, and she looked at the Tsarevich with a mocking smile, and all the Boyars, the Grandees, and the Councillors who were in the palace looked intently at the Tsarevich. And the Tsarevich said to the thrice-wise Helena: "Thy slipper is very fine, but 'tis no good at all unless it have a fellow. Well, here it is, and I give thee the other, which is exactly like it." And he drew out of his pocket the slipper, and placed it by the side of the other one. The whole palace heaved a great "Oh!" The Boyars, Grandees, and Councillors exclaimed with one voice: "Thou art indeed worthy, O Tsarevich, to wed our Tsarevna, the thrice-wise Helena."—"Not so quick, please," cried the Tsarevna; "let us see what he'll make of the second task. I shall await thee to-morrow in this self-same place, Tsarevich, and this is my task for thee: I shall have an unexplainable somewhat disguised in feathers and in stones; bring thou also just such another unknown, somewhat disguised in just such feathers and stones." The Tsarevich bowed and went out, looking much blacker than the evening before. "Well," thought he, "now indeed my shoulders will not support my head very much longer." And again Ivan the merchaut's son met him and consoled him with a friendly smile: "Come, Tsarevich, wherefore grieve? Pray to God and lie down to sleep, the morning is wiser than the evening." Ivan made the Tsarevich lie down, then he quickly took his invisible cap, darted into the palace, and arrived just in time to hear the Tsarevna give this command to her favourite servant: "Go into the fowl-yard and bring me hither a duck." Off went the servant to the fowl-yard and Ivan after her; she put a duck under her arm, but Ivan hid a drake in his bosom, and they came back the same way. The thrice-wise Helena again sat down at her little table, took the duck, adorned its wings with ribands and its little tail with amethysts, and fastened a necklace of pearls round its neck; and Ivan saw it all, and did just the same to his drake.

The next day the Tsarevich again went up to the palace, and again all the Boyars and Grandees were assembled there; again there was a crash of music, and the doors of the inner chambers opened, and the thrice-wise Helena came forth strutting along like a pea-hen. Behind her came the maids of honour bearing a golden dish, and they all saw that upon this dish beneath the white cloth some living thing was moving about. Softly, very softly, the Tsarevna raised the cloth from the dish, took out the duck, and said to the Tsarevich: "Well, didst thou guess my riddle?"—"How could I help guessing it?" replied the Tsarevich, "there's nothing so very knowing in such a task as that," and forthwith he put his hand into his cap and drew out his dressed-up drake.

All the Boyars and Grandees cried "Oh!" and with one voice exclaimed: "Well done, young hero Tsarevich! Thou art indeed worthy to take Helena the thrice-wise to wife." But Helena the thrice-wise knit her brows and said: "Stop a bit! Let him first fulfil my third task. If he be such a hero, let him fetch me three hairs from the head, and three hairs from the beard, of my grandfather, the Sea-king, and then I am ready to be his wife." The Tsarevich returned home gloomier than an autumn night: he would look at nothing and speak to nobody. "Don't fret, Tsarevich!" whispered Ivan the merchant's son in his ear, and he seized his invisible cap, and was in the palace in a trice, and saw the thrice-wise Helena sitting in her state-coach and preparing to drive to the blue sea. And our Ivan, in his invisible cap, took his seat in the very carriage, and the fiery horses of the Tsar carried them in hot haste to the blue sea.

So the thrice-wise Helena arrived at the blue sea, sat under a rock by the shore on a large stone, turned her face to the blue sea, and began to call her dear grandad the Sea-king. The blue sea boiled as in a storm, and despite a great calm, the depths of the sea were disturbed by a huge wave; a crest of silvery foam worked its way up, rolled along the shore as if caressing it, broke up gradually on the golden beach, scattering crystal jets and pearly shells on the shore, and there rose out of the water, up to the waist, the old, old grandfather. On his head heaps and heaps of gray locks sparkled like silver in the sun, dripping wet, and great tufts of hair hung over his brows; but his face was covered with a thick, thick golden beard like moss; he rode up to the breast in a broad big wave which swept over his shoulders and hid his body to the waist. The ocean grandfather leaned against a stone with his goose-like paws, looked with his green eyes into the eyes of the thrice-wise Helena, and cried: "Hail, grand-daughter of my desires. 'Tis a long time since I have seen thee; 'tis a long time since thou hast visited me. And now, please, comb my little head for me." And he leaned his unkempt head against the knee of his granddaughter, and dozed off into a sweet sleep. But the thrice-wise Helena began smoothing her grandfather's hair and winding his gray locks round her fingers to curl them, and whispering soft words in her grandfather's ear, and lulling him to sleep with gentle songs; and as soon as she saw that her grandfather was asleep she tugged three silver hairs out of his head. But Ivan the merchant's son, slipping his hand below hers, wrenched out a whole handful. The grandfather awoke, looked at his granddaughter, and said sleepily: "Art thou mad? It hurts me horribly!"—"Pardon, dear grandfather," said the thrice-wise Helena, "but it's such a long time since I did thy hair, that it is quite tangled." But the grandfather did not hear her to the end; he was already snoring, and shortly afterwards the Tsarevna pulled three golden hairs out of his beard. Ivan the merchant's son thought, "I must have some of that too," seized the grandfather by the beard, and tore out a good piece of it. The sea-grandfather roared aloud, awoke from his sleep, and dived into the depths like a bucket—only bubbles remained behind.

Next day the Tsarevna entered the palace and thought: "The Tsarevich really will fall into my clutches now." And she showed the Tsarevich the three golden hairs and the three silver ones: "Well, Tsarevich, hast managed to pick up such wonderful things as these?"—"Well, Tsarevna, that's a lot to boast of, I must say! Why, I'll give thee whole handfuls of such rubbish if thou wilt." And the whole palace resounded with cries of amazement when the Tsarevich drew from his breast the grandfather's hairs. The thrice-wise Helena was very wroth; she rushed off to her bedroom, looked into her magic books, and saw that it was not the Tsarevich who was so knowing, but his favourite servant, Ivan the merchant's son. She returned to her guests and said in soft and wheedling tones: "Thou hast not guessed my riddles and done my tasks of thine own self alone, Tsarevich, but thy favourite servant Ivan has helped thee. I should like to look at the good youth. Bring him to me quickly."—"I have not one servant but twelve servants, Tsarevna."—"Then bring him hither whose name is Ivan!"—"They are all called Ivan." —"Then let them all come," said she, but she thought to herself: "I'll pick out the guilty party, I know." The Tsarevich sent for his servants, and the twelve youths appeared at court. They were all of one face and one stature; their voices were all alike, and there was not a hair's difference between them. "Which among you is the biggest?" And they all cried with a loud voice: "I am the biggest, I am the biggest!"—"Well," thought Helena, "I can't catch you this way, but I'll manage it somehow." And she bade them bring eleven common drinking-cups, but the twelfth of pure gold; she filled the drinking-cups full with good wine, and gave them to the good youths to drink. But not one of them would look at the common cups, and all stretched out their hands towards the golden cup, so in struggling for it they only made a great clamour, and all the wine was spilled. The Tsarevna perceived that her artifice had failed, so she invited all the servants of the Tsarevich to pass the night at the palace. All the evening she gave them as much as they could eat and drink, and then she gave them soft downy beds to lie upon. And when all the good youths were sound asleep, then the thrice-wise Helena came to them in their bedroom, looked into her magic book, and immediately discovered which of them was Ivan the merchant's son. Then she drew out her penknife and cut off the lock of hair over his left temple, and she thought to herself: "By that mark I shall know you in the morning and have you punished." But in the morning, Ivan the merchant's son awoke before them all, clapped his hand to his head, and saw that he was shorn of his lock. He immediately rose from his bed and awoke all his comrades: "Quick, my brothers! take your knives and shear off your locks." In an hour's time they were summoned to the presence of the thrice-wise Helena. The Tsarevna looked and saw that all of them had their locks shorn off. Full of rage, she seized her magic book, pitched it into the fire, called the Tsarevich to her, and said to him : " I'll be thy wife, make ready for the wedding !" And the Tsarevich sent for his good youths, and said to Ivan : " Go to my sister and bid her make ready everything for the wedding." Ivan went to the Tsarevna, told her of her brother, and gave her his command. " I thank thee, thou good youth and faithful servant, for thy services," said the Tsarevich's sister to Ivan, " but say now, how shall I reward thee ?"—" How shalt thou reward me ? " answered Ivan the merchant's son ; " why, bid them put me again in my old dungeon." And do what the Tsarevna would to persuade him, he insisted upon it.

The Tsarevich and his bride arrived, and the Boyars, the Grandees, and the festal guests came out to meet them, wished them health and happiness, and presented them with bread and salt, and there were so many people pressed together that you could have walked on their heads. " But where is my faithful servant Ivan ? " asked the Tsarevich ; " how is it I do not see him here ? " The Tsarevna answered him : " Thou thyself hadst him put into a dungeon because of a certain dream."—" What ! surely this is never the same person ! "—" It's the very same ; I only let him out for a time to go and help thee." The Tsarevich bade them bring Ivan to him, threw himself on his neck, burst into tears, and begged him not to think evil of him. "But dost thou know, O Tsarevich," said Ivan, "that I did not tell thee this dream of mine because I saw beforehand in my slumbers all that has now happened to thee. Judge now thyself and tell me, wouldst thou not have thought me half mad if I had told thee all?" And the Tsarevich rewarded Ivan, and made him the greatest in the realm after himself; but Ivan wrote to his father and his brother, and they all lived together and had no end of good things, and lived happily ever after.

TWO OUT OF THE KNAPSACK.

THERE was once an old man whose wife was exceedingly quarrelsome. The old man had no rest from her day or night; she nagged and nagged at him at every little trifle, but if the old man ventured to gainsay *her* in anything, she immediately caught up a broomstick, or something else, and chased him out of the kitchen. The old man had only one consolation; he would leave his old woman and go into the fields to set snares and bird-traps, hang them up on the branches of all the trees, and entice into his snares every bird that God has made, and so he would bring home a great booty, and give his old woman enough to last her for a whole day, or even two, and then he would for once enjoy a day in peace.

One day he went out into the fields and set his snares, and caught in them a crane. "What a stroke of luck!" thought the old man; "when I take home this crane to my old woman and we kill and roast it, she won't row me for a long time." But the crane guessed his thoughts, and said to him with a human voice: "Don't take me home and kill me, but let me go and live at liberty as before; thou shalt be dearer to me than my own father, and I will be as good as a son to thee." The old man was amazed at these words and let the crane go.

But when he returned home with empty hands, the old woman nagged at him so frightfully that he dared not go into the house, but passed the night in the courtyard beneath the staircase. Very early in the morning he went out into the fields, and was just about to lay his snares when he saw the crane of the evening before coming towards him, holding in its long beak a sort of knapsack. "Yesterday," said the crane, "thou didst set me free, and to-day I bring thee a little gift. Say 'thanks' for it. Just look at it!" It placed the knapsack on the ground and cried: "Two out of the knapsack!" And whence I know not, but out of the knapsack leaped two youths, brought oaken tables, covered them with dishes, and on them was flesh and fowl of every description. The old man ate his fill of such delicacies as it had never been his luck to see all his life even from afar; he ate and drank without stopping, and would only rise from the table when the crane cried: "Two into the knapsack!" And the tables with all the flesh and fowl were as if they had never been. "Take this knapsack," said the crane, "and give it to thy old woman." The old man thanked him and went home. But all at once the desire seized him to brag about his booty to his godmother. So he went to his godmother, inquired after the healths of herself and her three daughters, and said: "Give me a little supper, according as God has blessed thee!" The godmother put before him what was on the stove, curtseyed, and bade him fall to. But the godson turned up his nose and said to the godmother: "Thine is sorry fare! Why I have as good as that when I'm on the road. I'll stand treat to thee."—"Very well, do so." The old man immediately brought out his knapsack, placed it on the ground, and the moment he cried: "Two out of the knapsack!" two youths, whence they came I know not, leaped out of the knapsack, placed the oaken tables, covered them with carved dishes, and placed upon them all sorts of flesh and fowl, such as the godmother had never seen from the day of her birth. The godmother and her daughters ate and drank their fill, and her thoughts were not good; she meant to deprive her godson of his knapsack by subtlety. And she began flattering her godson, and said to him: "My dear little dovey godson, thou art tired to-day, wilt thou not stop and have a bath?

We have everything handy to warm the bath-room for thee." The godson did not say no to a bath, hung up his knapsack in the hut, and went into the bath-room to bathe. But the godmother immediately bade her daughters sew together in hot haste just such another knapsack as the old man's, and when they had finished it, she foisted her knapsack on the old man, and took his knapsack for herself. The old man noticed nothing, and went home cheerily-cheerful; he sang songs and whistled all the way, and no sooner did he get home than he cried to his old woman: "Wife, wife, congratulate me upon the gift which I have got from the son of the crane!" The old woman looked at him and thought: "You've been drinking somewhere to-day, I know; I'll give you a lesson!" The old man when he got into the hut immediately placed his knapsack in the middle of the floor and cried: "Two out of the knapsack!" But out of the knapsack came nobody at all. A second time he cried: "Two out of the knapsack!" And again there was nobody. The old woman when she saw this let loose the full flood of her abuse upon him, flew at him like a whirlwind, caught up a wet mop on her way, and it was as much as he could do to escape from her and dash out of the hut.

The poor fellow fell a-weeping, and went to the self-same spot in the fields, thinking: "Perhaps I may meet the crane and get another such knapsack from him!" And indeed the crane *was* there, and was waiting for the old man with just such another knapsack. "Here is just such another knapsack, and it will be of as good service as the former one." The old man bowed to the very girdle and ran off home at full speed. But on the way a doubt occurred to him: "If now this knapsack be not quite the same as the other one, I shall get into a mess again with my old woman—and this time I shall not be able to hide my head from her even under the ground. Come along then: 'Two out of the knapsack!'" Immediately two young men leaped out of the knapsack with long sticks in their hands and began to belabour him, crying: "Don't go to thy godmother; don't be fooled by honeyed words!" And they kept on beating the old man till he bethought himself to say: "Two into the knapsack!" Then the young men hid themselves in the knapsack. "Well," thought the old man, "I cracked up the other knapsack to my godmother like a fool, but I shall not be a fool if I crack up this to her also. I wonder if she would like to filch this one from me also? She'd thank me on the other side of her mouth." So he went quite cheerily to his godmother, hung up the knapsack on the wall, and said: "Pray, heat me a bath, godmother."—"With pleasure, godson."

The old man got into the bath and had a good wash, staying as long as he could. The godmother called her daughters, placed them behind the table, and said: "Two out of the knapsack." And out of the knapsack leaped the young men with the long sticks and began beating the godmother and crying: "Give the old man back his knapsack." The godmother sent her eldest daughter to the old man and said: "Call our godson out of the bath; say that these *two* are beating me to death." But the godson replied out of the bath: "I have not finished bathing yet!" The godmother sent her youngest daughter, but the godson replied out of the bath: "I have not washed my head yet!" But the two youths kept beating the godmother all the time and saying: "Give back the old man's knapsack!" The godmother's patience was quite tired out, and she bade her daughters bring the stolen knapsack, and throw it to the old man in the bath-room. Then the old man got out of his bath and cried: "Two into the knapsack!" And the young men with the long sticks were no more.

Then the old man took both the knapsacks and went home. He approached the house and again began crying: "Congratulate me, wife, on the gifts I have got from the son of the crane!" The old woman flared up at once and got her broom ready.

But the old man when he came in, cried: "Two out of the knapsack!" and immediately the tables appeared before the old woman, and the two young men placed on the tables flesh and fowl in abundance. The old woman ate and drank her fill, and became quite mild and tender. "Well, dear little hubby, I'll thwack thee no more." But the old man after dinner took this knapsack and put it away, and unexpectedly got out the other, and placed it on the bench in the hut. The old woman wanted to see for herself how the old man's knapsack set to work, so she cried: "Two out of the knapsack!" Immediately the two young men with the long sticks popped out, and fell to beating the old woman, crying all the time: "Don't beat thy old man! Don't curse thy old man!" The old woman screeched with all her might, and called to her old man to help her. The old man took pity on her, came into the hut, and said: "Two into the knapsack!" and the two disappeared into the knapsack.

From henceforth the old man and the old woman lived together in such peace and quietness that the old man is always praising his old woman to the skies, and so this story ends.

THE STORY OF MARKO THE RICH AND VASILY THE LUCKLESS.

Not in our time, but a long time ago, in a certain realm, lived a very rich merchant, Marko by name, and surnamed the Rich. Cruel and hard was he by nature, greedy of lucre and unmerciful to the poor. Whenever the lowly and the needy came begging beneath his window he sent his servants to drive them away, and let loose his dogs upon them. There was only one thing in the world he loved, and that was his daughter, the thrice-fair Anastasia. To her only he was not hard, and though she was only five years old, he never gainsaid her one of her wishes, and gave her all her heart's desire.

And once on a cold frosty day, three gray-haired men came under the window and asked an alms. Marko saw them, and ordered the dogs to be let loose. The thrice-fair Anastasia heard of it, and implored her father and said: "My own dear father, for my sake don't drive them away, but let them pass the night in the cattle-stall." The father consented, and bade them let the poor old beggar-men into the cattle-stall for the night. As soon as every one was asleep Anastasia rose up, made her way on tiptoe to the stall, climbed up into the loft, and looked at the beggars. The old beggar-men were crouching together in the middle of the stall, leaning on their crutch-staves with their wrinkled hands, and over their hands flowed their gray beards, and they were talking softly among themselves. One of the old men, the oldest of them all, looked at the others and said: "What news from the wide world?" The second one immediately replied: "In the village Pogoryeloe,[1] in the house of Ivan the Luckless, a seventh son is born; what shall we call him, and with what inheritance shall we bless him?" And the third old man, after meditating a little, said: "We'll call him Vasily, and we'll enrich him with the riches of Marko the Rich, under whose roof we are now passing the night." When they had thus said they prepared to depart, bowed low to the holy ikons, and with soft footsteps prepared to depart from the stall. Anastasia heard all this, went straight to her father, and told him the words of the old men.

Marko the Rich thought deeply over it. He

[1] Burnt down.

thought and thought, and he went to the village Pogoryeloe. "I'll find out for certain," thought he, "whether such a babe really has been born there." He went straight to the priest and told him all about it. "Yes," replied the priest, "yesterday we had a babe born here, the son of our poorest serf; I christened him Vasily, and luckless he certainly is; he is the seventh son in the family, and the eldest son of the family is only seven years old; the sons of this poor peasant are wee, wee little things; there is next to nothing to eat and drink there; and such hunger and want is in the house that there's none in the village who will even stand sponsor." At this news the heart of Marko the Rich began to ache. Marko thought of the unhappy youngster, declared he would be godfather, asked the priest's wife to be godmother, and bade them make ready a rich table; and they brought the little fellow, christened him, and sat down and feasted.

At the banquet Marko the Rich spoke friendly words to Ivan the Luckless, and said to him: "Gossip, thou art a poor man, and cannot afford to bring up thy son; give him to me; I will bring him up among well-to-do people, and I will give into thy hand at once for thine own maintenance one thousand rubles." The poor man thought the matter over, and then shook hands upon it. Marko gave gifts to his fellow-sponsor, took the child, wrapped him in fox furs, put him in his carriage, and drove homewards. They had got some ten versts from the village when Marko stopped the horses, took up the child, went to the brink of a great precipice, whirled the child over his head, and pitched it down the precipice, exclaiming: "There you go, and now take possession of my goods if you can!"

Shortly after that some merchants from beyond the sea chanced to be travelling by the self-same road; these merchants brought with them twelve thousand rubles which they owed to Marko the Rich. They passed along by the side of the precipice, and they heard within the precipice the crying of a child. They stopped their horses, went to the precipice, and looked amongst the snowdrifts of the green meadows, and on a meadow a little child was sitting and playing with flowers. The merchants took up the child, wrapped him round with furs, and went on their way. They came to the house of Marko the Rich, and told him of their strange discovery. Marko immediately guessed that the matter concerned his own little serf boy, and he said to the merchants: "I should very much like to look at your foundling; if you will give him to me out and out I'll forgive you your debt to me." The merchants agreed, gave the child to Marko, and departed. But Marko that same night took the child, put it in a little cask, tarred it all over, and threw it into the sea.

The cask sailed and sailed along, and at last it came to a monastery. The monks happened to be on the shore just then; they were spreading out their fishing-nets to dry, and all at once they heard the crying of a child. They guessed that the crying came from the cask, and they immediately seized the cask, broke it open, and there was the child. They took the child to the abbot, and as soon as the abbot heard that the child had been cast upon the shore in a cask, he decided that the youngster's name should be Vasily, and that he should be surnamed the Luckless. And henceforth Vasily lived in the monastery till he was sixteen years old, and he grew up fair of face, soft of heart, and strong in mind. The abbot loved him because he learned his letters so quickly that he was able to read and sing in the church better than all the others, and because he was deft and skilful in affairs. And the abbot made him sacristan.

And it happened that once Marko the Rich was travelling on business, and came to this very monastery. The monks treated him with honour as a rich guest. The abbot commanded the sacristan to run and open the church; the sacristan ran at once, lit the candles, and remained in the choir, and read and sang. And Marko the Rich asked the abbot if the young man had dwelt there long, and the abbot told him all about it. Marko began to think, and it struck him that this could be no other than his serf-boy. And he said to the abbot: "Would that I could lay my hands upon such a smart young fellow as your sacristan, I would place all my treasures beneath his care; I would make him the chief overseer of all my goods, and you know yourselves what goods are mine." The abbot began to make excuses, but Marko promised the monastery a donation of ten thousand rubles. The abbot wavered; he began to consult the brothers, and the brothers said to him: "Why should we stand in Vasily's way? let Marko the Rich take him and make him his overseer." So they deliberated, and agreed to send away Vasily the Luckless with Marko the Rich.

But Marko sent Vasily home in a ship, and wrote to his wife this letter: "When the bearer of this letter reaches thee, go with him at once to our soap-works, and when thou dost pass the great boiling cauldron, shove him in. If thou dost not do this I will punish thee severely, for this youth is my prime enemy and evil-doer." Vasily duly arrived in port and went on his way, and there met him in the road three poor old men, and they asked him: "Whither art thou going, Vasily the Luckless?"—"Why, to the house of Marko the Rich, I have a letter for his wife."—

"Show us the letter," said the old men. Vasily took out the letter and gave it them. The old men breathed on the letter and said: "Go now, and give the letter to the wife of Marko the Rich—God will not forsake thee."

Vasily came to the house of Marko the Rich and gave the letter to his wife. The wife read Marko's letter, and called her daughter, for she could not believe her own eyes, but in the letter was written as plain as plain could be: "Wife, the next day after thou dost receive this my letter, marry my daughter, Anastasia, to the bearer, and do so without delay. If thou doest it not thou shalt answer to me for it." Anastasia looked at Vasily, and Vasily stared at her. And they dressed Vasily in rich attire, and the next day they wedded him to Anastasia.

Marko the Rich came home from the sea, and his wife with his daughter and son-in-law met him on the quay. Marko looked at Vasily, fell into a furious passion with his wife, and said to her: "How darest thou wed our daughter away without my consent?" But the wife replied: "I dared not disobey thy strict command!" and she gave the threatening letter to her husband. Marko read the letter, and saw that the handwriting was his own if the intention was not, and he thought to himself: "Good! thrice hast thou escaped ruin at my hands, but now I will send thee where not even the ravens shall pick thy bones."

Marko lived for a month with his son-in-law and treated him and his daughter most kindly; from his face nobody could have thought that he nourished evil thoughts against him in his heart. One day Marko called Vasily to him and said to him: "Go to the land of Thrice-nine, in the Empire of Thrice-ten, to Tsar Zmy[1]; twelve years ago he built a palace on my land. Thou therefore take rent from him for all the twelve years, and get news from him concerning my twelve ships, which have been wrecked about his kingdom for the last three years, and have left no trace behind them." Vasily dared not gainsay his father-in-law, but prepared for his journey, took leave of his young wife, took a sack of sweetmeats as provision by the way, and set out.

He went on and on, and whether it was long or short, far or near, matters not, but anyhow at last he heard a voice which said: "Vasily the Luckless, whither art thou going? is thy journey far?"—Vasily looked around him on all sides and answered: "Who called me? speak!"—"'Tis I, the old leafless oak, and I ask thee whither art thou going, and is thy journey far?"—"I am going to Tsar Zmy to collect arrears of rent for the last twelve years." And again the oak

[1] Serpent.

said to him: "If thou arrivest in time, think of me and ask him: here the old leafless oak has been standing all these three hundred years, and is withered and rotten to the very root—how much longer must he be tormented in this wide world?" Vasily listened attentively, and then went further. He came to a river and sat in the ferry-boat, but the old ferryman looked at him and said: "Is thy journey before thee a long one, Vasily the Luckless?"—Vasily told him. "Well," said the ferryman, "if thou art in time, remember me, and say to him I have been ferrying here all these thirty years; how much longer, I should like to know, shall I have to go backwards and forwards?"— "Good!" said Vasily, "I will say so."

He went on to the straits of the sea, and across the straits a whale-fish was lying stretched out, and a road marked out by posts went across its back, and people passed to and fro there. When Vasily stepped on to the whale, the whale-fish spoke to him with a man's voice and said: "Whither art thou going, Vasily the Luckless, and is thy journey far?" Vasily told it everything, and the whale-fish said again: "If thou art in time, remember me; the poor whale-fish has been lying across this sea these three years, and a road marked out by posts goes across its back, and horse and foot trample into its very ribs, and it has no rest night or day; how much longer, pray, is it to lie here?"—"Good!" said Vasily, "I will say so," and went on further.

Vasily went on and on, and he came to a broad green meadow. In the meadow stood a gigantic palace; the white marble walls glistened, the roof shone like a rainbow, and was covered with mother-of-pearl, and the crystal windows burned like fire in the sun. Vasily entered the palace; he went from room to room, and marvelled at the indescribable wealth of them. He went into the last room of all, and saw a lovely damsel sitting on a bed. When she saw Vasily, she cried: "Is it Vasily the Luckless that has fallen into this accursed place?" Vasily told her everything, and why he had come, and what had befallen him in the way. And the damsel said to Vasily: "Not to take tribute wast thou sent here, but as food for the serpent, and to thine own destruction." Scarcely had she spoken these words than the whole palace trembled, and there was clanging and a banging in the courtyard. The damsel shoved Vasily into a coffer beneath the floor, locked him in, and whispered: "Listen to what I say to the Serpent." And with that she went to meet Tsar Serpent.

A monstrous serpent rolled into the room, and straightway got on to the bed and said: "I have been flying over the Russian land; I'm frightfully tired, and I want to go to sleep." The lovely damsel flattered him and said: "Everything is known to thee, O Tsar, and without thee I cannot interpret a very hard dream I have dreamed: wilt thou interpret it for me?"—"Well, out with it, quick!"—"I dreamt I was going along a road, and an oak tree cried to me, 'Ask the Tsar how long I am to stand here'!"—"It will stand till some one comes and kicks it with his foot, and then it will be rooted out and fall, and beneath it is a great quantity of gold and silver: Marko the Rich himself has not got as much."—"But then I dreamed that I came to a river, and the ferryman on the ferry-boat said to me: 'Shall I ferry here long'?"—"'Tis his own fault. Let him put the first who comes to him on the ferry-boat, and push him with the ferry-boat away from the shore, and he will change places with him, and ferry for evermore."—"And after that I came in my dreams to the sea, and crossed over it on a whale-fish, and it said to me: 'Ask the Tsar how long I am to be here'!"—"He must lie there till he has cast up the twelve ships of Marko the Rich, then he may go into the water, and his body will grow again."

All this the serpent said, and then turned over on its other side and fell a-snoring so loudly that all the crystal windows in the palace rattled. Then the damsel let Vasily out of the coffer, opened the garden-gate for him, and showed him the way. Vasily thanked her, and began his return journey.

He came to the straits of the sea where the whale-fish lay, and the whale-fish asked: "Did he say anything about me?"—"Take me over to the other side, and I'll tell thee." When he had crossed over, he said to the whale-fish: "Thou must bring up again the twelve ships of Marko the Rich, which thou swallowed three years ago." The whale-fish cleared its throat and brought up again all the ships quite whole and not a bit hurt, and in its joy leaped about so in the water that Vasily the Luckless, who was standing on the bank, suddenly found himself up to his knees in the sea. He went on further and came to the ferry. "Hast thou spoken about me to Tsar Serpent?" asked the ferryman. "I have; ferry me over first, and I'll tell thee." And as soon as he had crossed over, he said to the ferryman: "Whoever comes to thee after me, seat him in the ferry-boat and shove him from the bank, and he will have to ferry in thy place for ever and ever, but thou wilt be as free as the air." After that, Vasily came to the old leafless oak, kicked it with his foot, and the oak rolled over and the roots sprang out of the ground, and beneath the roots and beneath the stump there was gold and silver and precious stones without number. Vasily looked about him, and lo! up to the very place were sailing the twelve ships of Marko the Rich, the selfsame which the whale-fish had brought up; and in the foremost ship, in the very stern, stood the selfsame old men who had met Vasily when he had the letter to Marko the Rich, and saved him from destruction. And the old men said to Vasily: "Dost thou not see, Vasily, how the Lord has blessed thee?" And they got off the ship and went their way. And the sailors put all the gold and silver in the ships, and went home by sea.

Marko the Rich was more furious than ever. He bade them saddle his horse, and hastened off to Tsar Serpent to the land of Thrice-ten; he wanted to arrange matters with Tsar Serpent himself. When he came to the river, he got on to the ferry-boat, but the ferryman pushed him away from the shore, and there Marko remained as ferryman ever after, and there he is ferrying still. But Vasily the Luckless lived with his wife and mother-in-law, and was happy and prosperous and kind to the poor, and gave them meat and drink and clothed them, and disposed of all the wealth of Marko the Rich.

THE END.

Richard Clay & Sons, Limited, London & Bungay.